THE BOOK OF FIVE RINGS

The Warrior Series: Book Two

The Book of Five Rings

Miyamoto Musashi

D. E. Tarver

iUniverse Star
New York Lincoln Shanghai

The Book of Five Rings
Miyamoto Musashi

iUniverse Star
an iUniverse, Inc. imprint

For information address:
iUniverse, Inc.
2021 Pine Lake Road, Suite 100
Lincoln, NE 68512
www.iuniverse.com

ISBN: 0-595-30124-X

Printed in the United States of America

To my Mother, one of the strongest people I have ever known. I love you.

The path that leads to truth is littered with the bodies of the ignorant.

—Musashi

Contents

Preface

Of all the classic writings on strategy and martial arts, Musashi has always been my favorite. I read my first copy of his writings when I was a teenager, and I have read many copies and translations since. During all that time I studied martial arts and sword vigorously, and I have taught many students. I have noticed over the years, as my martial skills grew and my understanding opened, that I always seem to take something new away each time I read Musashi. In the mid-eighties, I started taking notes on the various things that would come to me while reading or teaching. Those notes became the foundation for this interpretation.

Even now as I read *The Book of Five Rings*, I am completely amazed at the astounding insight and pure genius of Miyamoto Musashi. Every time I think I have learned my last lesson from him, I find that my grasp of his teaching is still infantile. Musashi has a way of cutting through all the fluff and getting to the heart of the matter. He stated his opinion and left it for the diligent student to understand, and diligence is the key. The first time I read the book I thought that it was nice. By my third or fourth reading I thought it was deep. By the ninth or tenth time, I thought it was unobtainable. By now, which must be the ninetieth time, I see it as a pure work of genius. I have no doubt that Musashi was every bit as great as his reputation, if not more so.

I encourage you to approach this book the way you would a Masters Degree program. It is a lifelong study. If you read it once and toss it aside, you will fulfill Musashi's statement that most people would rather avoid truth than pursue it. In fighting for your life, statements like, "Everyone's opinion is equal" and "This is truth to me, but truth to you may be different" are irrelevant. There is only living and dying, and if you are wrong you are dead. Musashi said, "Truth is not what you want it to be; it is what it is, and you must bend to its power or live a lie." The more I study his writings and strive to attain higher levels of enlightenment, the more I find that statement to be true. Once I accepted that idea, my understanding grew immensely.

I encourage you to take any mindset you want when you begin this study, but be open and ready to change your opinion as truth presents itself to you. If you are stuck in the mindset of your education, your culture, your religion, or what your mother told you, then you will only gain enlightenment to the extent that you are willing to accept it. Enlightenment is available to every open mind, but a closed mind will remain in the dark. Strip away all expectations and all preconceived ideas of how things are. Accept truth as it comes to you. If you do not believe in truth, you will not get very far, and that is truth. Fire burns, and if you can accept that you can build on the knowledge and grow. I know that sounds simple, but I have been constantly surprised at how some people argue even that. But, like Musashi said, anyone can argue—anyone can spout words no matter how silly they may be—but few really get results.

I don't want to belabor that point, but on some level I now consider you one of my students, and I want to encourage you in the best way I can. Be open. Be honest with yourself. Accept truth. Never stop searching for truth. Always strive to do your best at anything you set your mind to. This is the way of the warrior, and if you would follow the warrior's path in your business, your study of martial arts, or your life's philosophy, you must accept truth as your friend.

Good luck. May Heaven favor you and God bless you. If you are a warrior, salutations.

D.E. Tarver

Japan's Warrior Climate

Many today look back on the life of Miyamoto Musashi and see a vicious cold-blooded killer bent on making a name for himself at the expense of others' lives. All in all, that is true; but we should judge Musashi by the times he lived in and not by our own.

Japan prior to Musashi had been a place of constant war and strife. The birth of the samurai took place in the Heian Period (or, at least most scholars think so). During this time, many powerful clans banded together for self-protection and began to hire armed guards to protect their families and land. Before long, every clan had their own army of samurai (samurai means "one who serves"). When clans clashed, their samurai would go into action and earn their pay. Over time, the samurai became a class of citizen, and one could become a samurai only by being born into a samurai family. No one born a samurai would ever want to become a merchant, and he could not become a noble, so he was stuck at one level of citizenship for his entire life. The higher he could rise within that class, the better he could provide for his family.

It doesn't take a lot to understand that a warrior who can kill ten people in battle is worth more than one who can kill only one or two. Therefore, this class of people became invaluable for their prowess in combat. The samurai children were prepared for their future by intense training and strict discipline, just as today our children are expected to learn academics. Our children are valued in society by the level of their education. For the most part, Harvard graduates make more money than graduates from community colleges. Likewise, proven warriors could command more respect and a higher position than those who were untested. There were no shortages of wars to fight in until 1600, when Tokugawa Ieyasu unified Japan at the battle of Sekigahara.

In 1603, Tokugawa Ieyasu was appointed shogun, and a time of peace came to a very restless warrior class. Proven warriors were still highly valued, but with no wars to fight, warriors had to fight each other in duels to prove their superiority. Dueling had started before 1603, but with continuous war halted, duels became more frequent. In 1605, a twenty-one-year-old Musashi set out to prove himself.

About Musashi

Miyamoto Musashi has long been considered by many to be the greatest swordsman that ever lived. Legends have a tendency to take on a life of their own, and in writing this short biography I found it nearly impossible to separate the facts from the folklore. However, there are two things we know to be unquestionable facts.

First, Musashi was a vicious, calculating warrior. He killed well over sixty men in duels even though he was far outnumbered at times. He developed his own style of sword fighting, the Nito Ichi Ryu or The School of Two Swords.

Second, he became one of the most famous artists in the history of Japan. He painted great works of art, wrote poetry, sculpted, practiced calligraphy, created fittings for swords, and generally excelled at any and everything to which he applied himself.

Taking these facts into account, I will try to recreate the life of the warrior poet as accurately as possible.

MIYAMOTO MUSASHI

Shinmen Musashi no Kami Fujiwara no Genshin was born in the village of Miyamoto in Mimasaka province around the year 1584 into a branch of the Harima warrior clan of Kyushu. Some sources say that his father divorced his mother, Omasa, and left him to her care, but arranged continuing visits. Others say that his mother died and his father abandoned him, and his uncle, a priest, raised him. Even at this early point it becomes hard to separate the facts from the fiction, but we can be relatively sure that he was not raised in a functional home.

Some sources credit his father for starting his education in sword fighting and *jitte* (a small side weapon), and others say his father either died or had no dealings with him. There is really no way to know which of these are true, but Musashi seems to have been fiercely independent throughout his life, both in his actions and in his way of thinking. It is therefore not stretching to think he may have taught himself how to use the sword.

Musashi was known as Ben no Suke around the village where he grew up. He was born with eczema due to congenital syphilis, which left him with severe scars over his head and face. Because of this he was never able to shave his head in the traditional topknot fashion popular among the samurai. Thus he was forced into independence and isolation from the first day of his life. As a result, he became extremely aggressive and had little regard for others, who he felt probably looked down on him anyway.

Not a lot is known about this period in his life, but we do know that he was very large for his age and for some reason he got into a fight with a warrior named Arima Kihei of the Shinto Ryu school of sword fighting at the age of thirteen. We don't know who the aggressor was, but many believe that the warrior had a sword and Musashi fought with a stick. Evidently, Musashi struck the man on the head with the stick and knocked him to the ground, and every time he tried to get up Musashi hit him again. Arima Kihei died where he had fallen, vomiting blood. Whether this was an agreed-upon duel or a street brawl no one really knows. At least one account goes like this:

> His opponent this day was one Arima Kihei, who was already famous in the area as an exponent of Shinto-Ryu Kenjutsu (the Shinto School of Swordsmanship). On the day before the duel, Musashi had passed by a sign that read, "Whoever wants to challenge me shall be accepted. Arima Kihei"—at this he added to the notice: "I will challenge you tomorrow" and left his name and address. That evening, a message arrived from Kihei accepting the challenge and setting the site of the duel. The next morning,

Musashi set out to the nominated site, sword in hand. The match went completely contrary to what was expected. The instant Musashi felled his adversary he became a minor sensation within the area.[1]

Even though Musashi lived in a world of violence and war, it seems amazing that at the age of thirteen he could defeat a grown warrior in a physical duel. Needless to say, it didn't take long for Musashi's reputation to spread. Soon after this bout he changed his name from Shinmen Musashi no Kami Fujiwara no Genshin to Miyamoto Musashi. This is a name that honored both his family and his birthplace.

At the age of sixteen he had his second duel, with Tadashima Akiyama, where he killed him. Again, not much is known about the circumstances surrounding this duel, but many believe it started as an open challenge from Tadashima Akiyama that Musashi answered.

Around this time, Musashi stopped bathing. Some sources say that he felt vulnerable while bathing, and some believe this was because he may have been attacked in a bathhouse. No one really knows why, and as far as I know Musashi himself never addressed the subject, but virtually everyone believes that he refused to bathe. Knowing Musashi's contempt for the society he lived in, a society that placed high value on an ideal of personal appearance that he could never achieve because of his scars, he may well have stopped all personal grooming to spite others. In any case, his appearance became more and more rugged and fierce as time passed.

On September 15, 1600, at 8:00 A.M., the forces of Ishida Mitsunari and Tokugawa Ieyuasu met on the foggy field of Sekigahara to fight over control of Japan. Ishida Mitsunari, the highest-ranking general of Toyotomi Hideyoshi, pledged his loyalty to Hideoshi's son after Hideyoshi's death in 1598. He brought his army of eighty thousand warriors against Ieyuasu's seventy-five thousand to claim the throne. Musashi, age sixteen, chose to fight for the Mitsunari army. The main part of the battle lasted only six hours and left seventy thousand dead. Ieyuasu crushed Mitsunari and took him captive. For the next three days, Musashi hid among the dead bodies while patrols of Ieyuasu samurai roamed the area looking for surviving Mitsunari warriors to execute. The Tokugawa family would control Japan for the next 265 years.

Not much is known about Musashi from that point until 1605 when, at the age of twenty-one, he set out for Kyoto to find duels and make a name for himself. No doubt there were many warriors on such pilgrimages around this time, and duels were fairly easy to find. These pilgrimages became very common in Tokugawa Japan, where, due to peace, out-of-work warriors had to find another way to make a name for themselves and earn a living. Some turned to farming, some to the arts, and some to commerce. However, many sought to make themselves famous so that they could gain appointment as sensei to one of the powerful clans. Musashi's travels seemed to be more for the purpose of improving his art and understanding of swordsmanship.

Musashi did not wait to gain any more experience; he went straight to the top. He issued a challenge to Yoshioka Genzaemon, one of the most notable swordsmen in Kyoto. The Yoshioka family ran a very successful kenjitsu school and had been teaching Japanese royalty for years. It is surprising that Genzaemon would even agree to the duel—after all, no one in Kyoto had ever heard of Musashi and his rank was barely above that of a peasant—but he did. The fight was scheduled for the next day at 5 A.M. Genzaemon arrived on time with several retainers. After two hours he grew impatient and sent his men to find Musashi. They found him still asleep in the inn. He sent his apology. Genzaemon had to wait another two hours before Musashi arrived. Genzaemon had become so furious that when he spotted Musashi strolling up to the fight area he charged with an attack. Musashi calmly sidestepped and struck Genzaemon on the head. One scholar recounts the entire episode:

> Immediately upon his arrival he visited the Yoshioka family and challenged Genzaemon, the family patriarch. Genzaemon accepted the challenge even though Musashi was an unknown and the

Yoshiokas were renowned swordsmen. The match was set for five o'clock the next morning at a field on the outskirts of Kyoto. Genzaemon brandished a wooden sword. He was accompanied by several retainers and arrived at the appointed spot at dawn, but Musashi was nowhere to be found. Genzaemon sent some of his disciples to investigate and see if Musashi was still at his inn. Indeed, Musashi was there, but he was asleep! This infuriated Genzaemon to no end and he had to wait two more hours before Musashi arrived. Musashi swaggered onto the field at high noon with a wooden sword in his hand. His appearance was calm and collected. An enraged Genzaemon made no attempt to conceal his anger. He immediately launched his attack against Musashi. Musashi blocked the attacks, parrying the blows. Although both received blows to the head, Musashi landed a crushing blow to Genzaemon's head, knocking him to the ground. Later, he regained consciousness to discover his right arm was broken in many places. Genzaemon was humiliated by the defeat. No sooner had the match ended than Denshishiro, Genzaemon's younger brother, challenged Musashi in order to preserve the family honor. Although Genzaemon was the head of the family, Denshichiro was considered to be a far better swordsman. He arrived at the appointed place with a steel sword that was over five feet in length with the intent of having Musashi's blood on it. Denshichiro was filled with confidence. He had seen Musashi's swordsmanship first-hand when his brother was defeated and thought he could beat him. Again, Musashi was late for the engagement but as soon as he arrived he launched a furious attack against Denshichiro with his *bokken*. Musashi quickly landed a crushing blow that killed Denshichiro on the spot! He later killed Matashichiro, the son of Genzaemon, who was only thirteen, by slashing him across the forehead, killing him instantly. As a result of the defeat of three of the Yoshioka family, Musashi's fame grew instantly in Kyoto.[2]

Musashi may have entered Kyoto as a poor, low-class nobody, but he left as a celebrated sword master. With his reputation racing ahead of him, Musashi wandered the countryside for the next eight years, engaging in over sixty duels. He faced many confrontations, sometimes extremely outnumbered, but never once lost—or did he? The following article records what could be Musashi's only loss.

If we can believe the legends—and there are more legends than facts concerning these two martial artists—the only person to beat Miyamoto Musashi in a duel was someone as outlandish and eccentric as he was. And to top it off, he did it with a wooden stick. In so doing, Muso Gonnosuke Katsuyoshi gave birth to a martial arts system that would elevate the humble wooden staff to one of the preeminent weapons of the *bugei* of Japan.

We know very little that can be verified about the actual life of Muso Gonnosuke, and the little that we do know must be tempered with the knowledge that much of what has been written has been colored and embellished by later writers to make for exciting reading. Nishioka Tsuneo, head of the Seiryukai organization, cautions that many of the legends purporting Gonnosuke to be a colorful braggart originated long after his actual lifetime. "We just don't know that much about him," Nishioka says.

In any case, records note that Gonnosuke's original family name was Hirano, and that he went by the given name of Gonbei early in his life. He was supposed to be a distant descendant of Kiso Kanja no Taiyu Kakumei, a retainer of the famous general Kiso Yoshinaka.

Gonnosuke studied the Tenshin Shoden Katori Shinto-ryu under Sakurai Ohsumi No Kami Yoshikatsu, then he studied the Kashima Jikishinkage-ryu, learning its secret method, called the "ichi no tachi." According to legends, Gonnosuke thereupon engaged in various duels throughout Japan to test his skills, never losing any of them until he met Miyamoto Musashi.

To be sure, there were wooden staff arts before Gonnosuke's time. The Tenshin Shoden Katori Shinto-ryu had *bojutsu* methods using the *rokushaku bo* (six-foot staff), as did the Sekiguchi-ryu, Bokuden-ryu, and Takeuchi-ryu (or, as it is alternatively called, Take-no-uchi-ryu). If we follow the lineage line charted in the *Bugei Ryuha Daijiten*, then Gonnosuke was a student of a teacher of the Tenshin Shoden Katori Shinto-ryu, which is why his style, the Shinto Muso (or Shindo Muso)-ryu contains the appellation Shinto (Way of the Gods).[3]

THE DUEL WITH MUSASHI AND MOUNT HOMAN

The first duel with Musashi occurred in Keicho 10 (1605), just five years after the Battle of Sekigahara put an end to most internal civil wars and heralded the start of the two-centuries-long Tokugawa peace. The event was supposed to have taken place in Akashi, Harima province. There are different versions of the first duel. A rather silly but entertaining one is concocted by Yoshikawa Eiji in the novel *Miyamoto Musashi*. However, the first records of such a duel is found in the *Kaijo Monogatari*, written in 1629. The gist of its version was subsequently published in the Jodo Kyoshi. The following is a synopsis of that episode:

There was a *heihosha* (martial artist) named Miyamoto Musashi. He engaged in duels from the age of sixteen and was in about sixty matches. In the sixth month, in Akashi, Harima province, he met Muso Gonnosuke, who was a six-foot-tall strapping warrior. Gonnosuke was armed with an *odachi* (a long sword), a two-layer overcoat with sleeves, and a *haori* with a large *hi no maru* (rising sun). On his lapels were written: "The best martial artist in the land" (*heiho tenka ichi*) and "Nihon Kaizan Muso Gonnosuke."

...Gonnosuke was surrounded by about six *deshi* followers who had accompanied him on a journey to Kyushu. He boasted to Musashi that no one was his equal. In his travels, he had apparently encountered Musashi's father, Shinmen Munisai, a master of the *jutte* (truncheon).

"I have seen your father's techniques, but I haven't seen yours," he said, goading Musashi.

(Shinmen) Miyamoto Genshin Musashi was irritated. He was in the middle of carving a willow branch and replied, "If you saw my father's techniques, I am no different."

Gonnosuke pressed the issue, badgering Musashi to show his martial arts off for the benefit of Gonnosuke's students.

"My *heiho* is not for display," Musashi snapped. "No matter how you attack me, I'll stop it. That's all there is to my *heiho*. Do what you will, with any technique."

Gonnosuke pulled out a four-*shaku* (a *shaku* is roughly equivalent to an English foot) wooden sword from a brocade bag. (To draw a comparison, the usual practice sword is but a little longer than two *shaku*.) He attacked Musashi without any formalities. Musashi stood up from his crouch. With what seemed to be very little effort, he forced Gonnosuke back across the tatami mat room with his willow branch and, pressing him against a wall, struck him lightly between the eyebrows.

Another slightly different version of that first duel appears in the *Honcho Bugei Koden*. The book was originally compiled in Shotoku 4 (1714). Watatani, in his edited and annotated version of the *Honcho Bugei Koden*, notes that the *Nitenki*, a compilation of Musashi's exploits by his followers, places the event in Edo, but this appears to be a later corruption. The earliest record of this duel appeared in the *Kaijo Monogatari*, but twenty-six years after Musashi's death, and it places the battle in Akashi.

The description of the duel in the *Honcho Bugei Koden* is more or less the same as in the *Kaijo Monogatari*, with some minor differences. In this version, Musashi was carving the willow branch into a toy bow used for sideshow games. It was a thin piece of wood only two *shaku* or so in length. Musashi invited Gonnosuke into a seven-and-a-half-mat room.

In actuality, it is probable that Musashi beat Gonnosuke by using his special two-swords technique (nito), trapping Gonnosuke's weapon in an x-block, or *juji dome*, with his long and short swords. Musashi was able to trap an opponent's weapon with the block, forcing the attacker to either give up or retreat and face an immediate counter-attack.

Gonnosuke must have been a large, strapping warrior if he wielded such a large *bokken* or *bo*. A wooden sword attributed to Gonnosuke at Chikuwa Shrine is over four *shaku*, nine *sun*, and two *bu* (over four feet) long. Gonnosuke's *jo*, if measured by the width of his outstretched hands held out to his sides, must have been a bit longer than the standard *jo* used nowadays.

Whatever the case may be, Gonnosuke lost the first duel. Mortified, he withdrew to Homangu, part of the Kamado Shinto Shrine atop Mount Homan, in Chikuzen province, (present-day Dazaifu, Fukuoka Prefecture) Kyushu. For thirty-seven days he meditated and performed rites of austerity. On the last night, while praying in front of an altar, he collapsed and had a divine vision.

In one version, a heavenly child appeared and said, "Holding a round log, know the *suigetsu* (an attack point on the body)."

The cryptic vision compelled Gonnosuke to whittle a short staff about four *shaku*, two *sun*, and one *bu* in length (128 cm). This was longer than the standard *tachi* long sword of that period, which was three *shaku*, two *sun*, and one *bu*, but shorter than the long *rokushaku bo*.

By taking advantage of the short staff's ability to shift rapidly in the hands of a skilled artist, Gonnosuke was able to beat Musashi in a second duel. It is unclear how Gonnosuke did that, but the use of the *jo* in present-day Shinto Muso-ryu practice might give us a hint. If a *jo* is blocked by a *juji-dome*, it is an easy matter to quickly flip the *jo* out of the block and in the same motion strike a *kyusho* (weak point) on the swordsman's body.

Gonnosuke also created a system of five-secret methods (hiden gyo-i) that incorporated all the techniques of his new *jo* style.

Gonnosuke managed to defeat Musashi without causing him great harm. Gonnosuke became martial arts instructor to the Kuroda clan, located in northern Kyushu. Muso Gonnosuke, profoundly changed by his encounter with Musashi and by the divine vision atop Mount Homan, had created a preeminent staff art, the Shinto (or Shindo) Muso-ryu jojutsu. The Heavenly Way of Muso's staff.

Whether this took place exactly as it is recorded here no one can really know. Musashi himself says he was never defeated, but if this took place it may well be that he chose to dismiss it. Even if he did lose this one duel it doesn't take away from the power of his legend or the lessons of his strategy.

In 1605, he defeated a spearman named Oku Hozion. Musashi defeated him in two duels using his short wooden sword. Evidently this was a very friendly contest, because Musashi and the priest of the temple became friends and he stayed with them for a while, training and engaging in evening conversations.

Musashi also fought and killed Shishido Baikin, a famous master of the kusari-gama—a sickle with a weighted chain attached. Musashi pulled a dagger and threw it at him and it stabbed him in the chest. While Baikin was startled, Musashi rushed him and cut him down. This duel shows that Musashi was committed to winning no matter what he had to do. Some have frowned on these sorts of tactics, but I for one agree with them. In life and death, there is only living and dying. Whether you think Musashi fought fairly or not, the fact is that Baikin died that day and Musashi lived on for many years. If you are not totally committed to winning then you will probably lose. Following the duel, Baikin's students attacked Musashi, but he counterattacked them so fiercely that they all ran to the winds.

Musashi then stopped in Izumo province to visit Lord Matsudaira. While he was there, he asked to fight Matsudaira's best kendo master. Lord Matsudaira consented and set the location for the duel in his garden. Musashi armed himself with two wooden swords while the kendo master used an eight-foot hexagonal wooden staff. Musashi attacked with so much power that he drove the Kendo master up the steps of the veranda, where he struck him on both arms with his wooden swords. Lord Matsudaira was so impressed that he asked Musashi to duel with him. Musashi agreed and drove Matsudaira up the veranda steps, and even broke his sword using the Fire and Stones cut. Lord Matsudaira was astounded and insisted that Musashi stay with him for a while and teach him.

Musashi's most famous duel took place in 1612, in Bunzen province, against Sasaki Kojiro. The lord of the province gave his consent for the duel to take place on a nearby island. Musashi again did not show up on time and retainers were sent to get him. He went to the appointed island by boat and made his weapon out of an ore as he approached. Once at the beach he jumped out of the boat and charged. Kojiro drew his sword and tossed the scabbard aside. Musashi shouted, "You will not need that again." Both warriors clashed head on, swinging their weapons simultaneously. Kojiro's sword actually cut Musashi's headband off his head, but Musashi's stick was a little quicker and he crushed Kojiro's skull. Kojiro died on the beach.

From about this point on, Musashi almost never used steel swords again. Instead, he preferred the challenge of using a stick against sharp swords. Musashi had become invincible and he knew it.

At this point, Musashi had become so comfortable with his skill that he started experimenting with different techniques. It was about this time that he first used his famous two-sword style that he wrote about in *The Book of Five Rings*. In Enmyo, he used two swords (some say steel, some say wooden) against Gunbei. The duel ended when Gunbei charged Musashi in a fit of rage and impaled himself on Musashi's short sword—which is hard to do on a wooden sword.

From 1614 to 1615, Musashi again experienced war on a large scale with the winter and summer siege of Osaka castle. No one really knows what his official duties were, but we can be sure that he was a perceptive student. Latter, in 1638, he served as an advisor to the shogun during the Shimabara Rebellion. His three experiences with large-scale warfare make his advice on war all the more credible.

Musashi believed that once you achieve enlightenment in strategy then you can see it in everything you do. He used this philosophy to engage in the arts and created some of the most impressive pieces of art in Japanese history. A true warrior poet, Musashi was able to completely commit himself to any endeavor he chose. His talents seem to have been endless, and in any age he is truly a Renaissance man.

Whether you like Musashi or not, he is certainly one of the most remarkable men in the history of the world.

A MUSASHI POEM

The master swordsman Miyamoto Musashi has expressed this serene and clear state of mind in the following poem:

> *"Kanryu taigetsu*
> *Saeru mizu no gotoshi"*

"Cold flow, still moon
Like clear water"

In this poem, Musashi speaks of the clarity, or *sae*, of pure water, evoking the purity of an unblemished mind. If water contains any impurities, it becomes muddy and unclear when it is disturbed as all the debris it contains rises to the surface. This agitated, impure water can be compared to *haru ki*. As the water becomes calm, the debris settles and the water becomes clear. This is *sumu ki*. *Saeru ki* is when all of the debris is gone. When there is nothing left to cloud the water, it will always be clear no matter what happens, because it is just water, with nothing else in it.[4]

With this clear state of mind, let us proceed.

The Book of Five Rings

D.E. Tarver
www.detarver.com

Musashi's Introduction

My name is Miyamoto Musashi. I am a warrior, born in the province of Harima. I am now sixty years old.

I have spent my entire life studying and refining the way of strategy. I killed first when I was just thirteen, and I have won in over sixty duels, never once losing in my entire life. I named my way of strategy the School of Two Swords, and I thought it best to share my teachings and to commit to history my way by my own hand. I have climbed the mountain Iwato in the Higo province of Kyushu. Before beginning, I have bowed down to give thanks for Heaven's Mercy and to honor the dead.

I devoted myself to understanding the way of conflict since my childhood. In my first real fight, when I was thirteen, I struck down Arima Kihei, a student of the Shinto school. At the age of sixteen I took the life of Akiyama, a very strong warrior of the Tajima province. When I was twenty-one I moved to the capital and fought with experts from every kind of strategy. I defeated them all, and never once did I fail.

From there I traveled through every province and challenged worthy opponents from every way of strategy, and I defeated them all. All of these things happened from the time I turned thirteen through my twenty-ninth year.

When I reached the age of thirty it came to me that I had not won because of any mastery on my own part. Maybe I had just been lucky, maybe it just came naturally to me, maybe it was a gift from Heaven, or maybe the other schools of strategy were simply lacking in some way. This caused a yearning for understanding in me, and I set forth to learn through meditation and study, day and night. I came to enlightenment twenty years later at the age of fifty.

Since that time I have had no need to study any other way or to have any teacher. Once enlightenment came through strategy, I understood other things as well.

I did not write this book using religious ideas or any particular philosophy, and I did not use examples from old military records. Instead, I take the brush in hand myself to explain my own experiences and to teach my own way. As I sit here it is 4:00 A.M. on the tenth day of the tenth month, 1643.

And so it begins.

The Book of Earth

Martial arts are a way of life for the warrior. Everyone from the commander to the foot soldier must be familiar with the arts of war and the way of strategy, although it is the commander's primary responsibility. There is no perfect strategy; therefore, no one can say that they have a complete understanding of it.

There are many paths one may take in life. There is the path of salvation by faith. There is the path of philosophy, or of education. There is the path of a poet, or of an artist. All people pursue paths of one type or another, and all people are inclined to believe one way or another. People are drawn to the path that brings them the most satisfaction. There are not many people who are drawn to the path of the warrior. The warrior stands alone.

A proper warrior must be versed in several paths. Not only must he devote his time and energy to perfecting his martial art, but he should also strive to master other paths as well. A warrior should be comfortable not only with the sword, but also with the brush. He should not only be able to take life, but he must be able to create beauty as well. Even those warriors who are not well-adapted to poetry or painting should strive for perfection in these areas.

It is generally believed that the path of the warrior is encumbered with death, both the deaths of his opponents and his preparation for his own inevitable death. The truth is that we all must die. It is the resolute end of us all, whether we are prepared or not. The only shame in death is dying for no reason. Many people from all paths of life have lain down their lives for honor or for the sake of a loved one. Under these circumstances we are all like warriors.

The real path of the warrior is the pursuit of excellence in all that they do. Whether you are writing poetry, painting, or drawing swords for combat, you must strive to be better than anyone else. Whether triumphing over a single opponent or winning wars with armies, the warrior's thoughts should remain first on serving his employer well and then on his own interest. The warrior's last priority should be making a name for himself. Some people believe that the path of the warrior and the study of the martial arts are only useful in the case of war. This is not so. If you attain enlightenment in the martial arts then all that you do will be enlightened and all that you teach to others will come from an enlightened mind.

Such is the way of strategy.

THE WAY OF STRATEGY

Everywhere that people have pursued the art of strategy a few have eventually become known as masters. You must study their lessons without stopping.

Many people who claim to be masters these days really only teach a few basic techniques in order to make a living. Take for example the Priest of Kashima and Kantori in Hitachi province, who recently opened their schools. They claim to have learned their martial arts from the gods, and they now travel all over the country teaching others.

The study of strategy has long been listed among the ten skills and seven arts most profitable to learn. Thus, if we are talking about strategy it can hardly be limited to the study of a few basic sword techniques. Even the art of the sword by itself cannot be learned by the study of techniques alone, much less the entire realm of strategy and military science.

Look around and you will find many people who sacrifice true martial arts for profit. They dance about and try to look flashy, making a commodity of themselves. They invent silly things to sell even if they are obviously useless, and they never stop and think about what they are doing. They claim that this school or that school is better based on nothing but how well they show off, and they are more concerned with making a profit by teaching rather than taking the time to learn. It's like separating the flower from the seed and valuing the flower more, even though it will quickly fade and the seed can give them many flowers. As they say, a little knowledge is a dangerous thing.

Generally speaking, there are four basic groups in life.

1. Laborers

2. Merchants

3. Craftsmen

4. Managers

LABORERS

The most common folk are the laborers. Laborers, such as farmers, possess many various tools and spend their lives watching for and in anticipation of changing seasons. Such is the way of a laborer.

MERCHANTS

Second is the merchant, such as the wine maker. They gather the ingredients and make their wine, then sell it for a profit. Whatever they sell, the merchant makes his living by trade at a premium. Such is the way of a merchant.

CRAFTSMEN

Third are the craftsmen, such as carpenters and architects. The craftsman has many tools at his disposal. He must be able to draw up plans for an entire project and then carry out construction accordingly. A craftsman must also calculate measurements accurately and be diligent at his craft. Such is the way of the craftsman.

MANAGERS

Managers, such as warriors, noblemen, and landowners, are the highest class. They control people and resources. Managers spend their time constructing or learning about various weapons that will give them the advantage over others. This is absolutely necessary. Failure to properly understand a weapon or to miss gaining the upper hand because of improper use of a weapon suggests shortcomings in a manager's ability.

Therefore, Laborers, Merchants, Craftsmen, and Managers are the four walks of life.

As a description, we use the word "house" to refer to many things. We often speak of noble houses, financial houses, military houses, and many others. I will use this metaphor to explain strategy as well. The word carpenter is written with the same Chinese character that could also read "master plan." If you want to understand strategy, read this very carefully. The lesson is the needle and you are the thread; let this image be in your mind constantly.

CARPENTRY AND THE WAY OF STRATEGY

The chief carpenter is responsible for organizing materials and resources and for the overall quality of work from those carpenters under him. He must know the building codes of the region, the laws of the city, and the expectations of the landowner for whom he is building the house. By reason of his trade, the chief carpenter must know how to build any and every type of dwelling and establishment, and he must know how to get his carpenters to construct these buildings properly. In this the chief carpenter is the same as a general.

Before the construction of a house starts, the lumber is sorted. Lumber that is beautiful, free from knots and strong, is used for support in the very front. Lumber that is not so beautiful and has some knots, but is nevertheless strong, is used for support in the back of the house, where no one will see it. Lumber that is beautiful and free of knots but not as strong is used for doorframes, doors, and lintels. Strong lumber can always be used discreetly in construction, even if it's not so beautiful, so long as care is taken, and the result will be a strong house. Even that lumber which is weak and knotted is used for scaffolding and later for firewood.

The chief carpenter gives out work assignments according to the ability of his men. He will assign some to work on the alcove, some to build the doorways and walls, some to construct the lintels and windows, and so forth. The less skilled the worker, the less responsibility he is given. Some will work on preparing lumber, and some will fetch supplies. It is in this way that the chief carpenter makes the best use of each worker, thus increasing productivity.

To build anything quickly and maintain quality means not being disorganized with anything. Know the dispositions of your men, understand their individual motivations, know how to offer proper incentive, and understand how to instill confidence. Never demand the unreasonable and offer encouragement when it is needed; these are the things a chief carpenter thinks about.

The principles of all strategy are the same.

THE WAY OF STRATEGY

Every carpenter is like a warrior in that he must clean and care for his own tools. He must insure that they are sharp and store them properly before carrying them around. The carpenter works under the command of the chief carpenter, making pillars and beams with an axe; he shapes floorboards and cabinets with a plane. He even carves elaborate decorations in the open for all to admire. The carpenter must calculate correctly and follow the blueprints perfectly. Such is the way of a carpenter. Those who apply themselves, work diligently, and study constantly can one day become chief carpenters themselves.

It is necessary for the accomplished carpenter to keep sharp tools and to care for them constantly. Then he can build small, elaborate shrines, writing tables, lanterns, cutting boards, and pot covers. Warriors are essentially the same as carpenters. You should meditate on this with deep consideration.

The test of a carpenter is that his work when finished is straight and smooth, not warped and misaligned. It should be well-planed and free of abrasion and should stand the test of time.

If you are sure you want to learn the way of strategy then you should ponder each of these things in great detail.

AN OVERVIEW OF THE FIVE SECTIONS OF THIS BOOK ON STRATEGY

For this book, I have taken the whole of my teaching on strategy and broken it into five sections. Each section is fully self-contained, like a circle or a ring, and they are titled respectively Earth, Water, Fire, Wind, and Emptiness.

EARTH

The first section, Earth, is where I lay the foundation for the proper way of thinking and explain the general philosophies of my way of strategy. If you do not look past simple technique you will never really understand strategy. For true understanding you must step back and look at the whole picture from the smallest things to the largest. It is like traveling a well-beaten path. If you only look at what is right in front of you, you will not see very far, but if you get a higher view point you can see the whole path and know where you are going.

WATER

The second section, Water, is where I compare the active mind to the fluidity of water. Water conforms to the shape of its container whether it is round or square, and water functions as a single body whether it is a single drop or an ocean. Water is clear blue in color, and likewise I want to explain my approach to strategy clearly.

The principles of strategy used to defeat a single opponent are the same principles used to defeat any opponent. The principles of strategy used in one-on-one combat are the same as the principles used when fighting whole armies. As water can be a drop or an ocean, so the strategist uses small things to construct great things, such as building a huge statue using a small model. This cannot really be explained with words; you must come to the understanding yourself. Understanding is not the same as education or knowledge. If you come to truly understand one thing you will understand the nature of everything. Things that are particular to my way of strategy are written in this section.

FIRE

The third section, Fire, is where I write about combat. Fire, whether large or small, is extremely fierce, and combat is the same way. Whether you are fighting a single opponent or leading an army, you must have the same spirit of fierceness. It is difficult because large bodies of people move slowly and are easy to follow, but a single individual can change positions quickly, on the spur of the moment, and can be hard to keep up with. You must consider this carefully.

Now consider fire. Small or large, fire can change positions abruptly and with no warning. You must strive to do likewise. Furthermore, you must adapt instantly to an opponent who does this. It is the very foundation of strategy to be able to adapt to any situation and continue fighting without losing heart. You gain this ability by practicing day in and day out with intensity.

WIND

The fourth section, Wind, is where I write about the teachings of all other schools. By using the word wind I mean to indicate old traditions, modern traditions, and traditions passed down through families.

Unless you understand what other schools are teaching, you will not be able to distinguish true thought from false thought. It is easy for the beginner to be lead astray and to follow teachings that are not true. Even if you deviate from the truth only slightly, in the end you will be far from the truth and not even know it. In strategy, especially with swords, you will not know if you are right or wrong until you kill your opponent or he kills you. No contest can ever reveal truth, only real combat. Thus, the path that leads to truth is littered with the bodies of the ignorant.

These days, when people think of martial arts they mostly think of simple fighting technique, and if you look at how some schools are teaching martial arts, it is understandable. My way of martial arts is completely different in that we follow a deeper principle. I explain this difference in the book of wind.

EMPTINESS

The fifth section, Emptiness, is where I consider nature. By emptiness I mean to describe the proper state of mind. Emptiness has no beginning, no end, and no stopping point. You learn all the techniques and principles of strategy, then you forget them and let the knowledge flow through you. Follow your natural instincts without debate. Move with the rhythm of any situation and adapt spontaneously. All of nature operates on this principle; only people complicate nature with thought. Do not misunderstand: thought is necessary in its place. You should think long and hard about all things, but at some point it is time to stop thinking and move to action. Take walking, for example. Watch the child as it struggles with all the thoughts associated with walking, movement, balance, timing, and so forth. Now consider yourself: walking requires no thought; you simply do it without thinking.

This is enlightenment, for even though you know all the principles, they do not bind you and you are free to let strategy happen. When you reach this point you will strike any opponent with proper timing and speed as naturally as you walk.

THE NAME TWO SWORDS

I call my way of strategy "One Mind-Two Swords." Let me explain why. In olden days, it was customary for a warrior to carry two swords at his side. One was called the long sword and the other simply sword. Later they became known as the long sword and the companion sword. It is not necessary to go into the details here of why this was so, just let it suffice to know that it was. Today, samurai still wear the two swords even though most of them do not really understand why. When fighting, they lay both hands on the long sword and ignore the other one. For this reason I named my style Two Swords so it would be clearly different from the start.

Now, the spear and the *naginata* are different matters entirely. These weapons are used where the sword is impractical and they require the use of both hands.

Even the beginners in my school start off by training with two swords, the long sword in one hand and the companion sword in the other. This seems awkward to them at first, but with continued practice they become comfortable and learn to move about freely. When your life is on the line you want every advantage you can get, and when you use both hands on one sword you cannot move freely from left to right. If you turn left, your right is left open; if you turn right your left is left open. No warrior should die with an unused weapon at his side. Using my method you will have every resource available to protect yourself on all sides.

Unlike the spear and *naginata*, you have a choice with the swords of using one or both. If you choose to use both hands you should consider all the situations that will be very awkward for you. Riding a horse, running, moving about quickly on rocky or uneven ground, or fighting in a crowd are all extremely difficult when you use two hands to hold a single sword. If you carry a bow, a spear or any other weapon in addition to the sword, you have to wield the sword with the one free hand. Therefore it is ridiculous to train any other way.

Because of armor and various situations, sometimes it is not possible to kill a man using a one-handed cut, and in this case you should make the killing cut with both hands. If you are properly trained, this should come naturally and require no thought. I start my students' training with a sword in each hand because I want them to be comfortable with it, but I also train them to adapt and to flow freely.

No matter what you study—the bow, the spear, walking, running, writing, or the swords—it will seem very difficult at first, and you may think you will never be able to do it properly. However, as time passes and you continue to practice you will become more accustomed to your field of endeavor and it will become easy. With time it requires no thought and becomes nothing but reflex.

Now, as far as the long sword goes, the beginner thinks only of speed and power. This is not always the best way, and the long sword is not always the best choice. Sometimes the short sword is better. I will explain this thoroughly in the Water section.

Using my strategy you can win with long swords or with short swords. I do not concern myself so much with the weapon as with the spirit. It is the fierce spirit of a warrior that cuts down his opponents. Therefore you should strive to gain the warrior's spirit and you will be victorious with long sword, short sword, or no sword at all. You will win because you will fight for victory using any means necessary to kill your opponent.

It is always advantageous to use two swords when fighting a mob by yourself or when taking prisoners, but these things cannot really be explained in writing. You must come to the understanding yourself.

The things in this book come from an enlightened viewpoint and require a lot of study. When you truly understand one thing, you will understand the nature of all things and there will be nothing you cannot see. Study this with all diligence day and night.

THE TERM MARTIAL ARTS

In the way of the warrior, after you reach a certain level of proficiency you are called a martial artist. As a martial artist, you may use the bow and be an archer, you may use the spear and be a spearman, or you may use the gun and be a marksman. It should follow that one who is proficient with the sword would be called a long swordsman or a short swordsman, but such is not the case. While all of these weapons are tools of the martial artist, it is taken for granted that any martial artist is comfortable with the sword. The sword is the icon for all of the martial arts.

If you are proficient with the sword then you are master of yourself and your environment. Understanding the sword is the beginning of strategy, and one with proper understanding can defeat ten men in combat. If one can be victorious against ten, then ten can be victorious against one hundred, and a hundred against a thousand, and so on. Thus, one man or an entire army will use my strategy the same way, so strategy is the very foundation of my martial arts.

Strictly speaking, in-depth studies of philosophy, religion, etiquette, or fine arts are not necessary to understand strategy. But if you have a true understanding of strategy you will see it in everything. You should study all things to broaden your life. You should specialize in several things to polish your life.

UNDERSTANDING WEAPONS IN STRATEGY

All weapons have their place. Regardless of the weapon, there is a time and a place where it is appropriate and the best tool of choice. You should strive to gain familiarity with all weapons but specialize in only a few.

Various circumstances require various tools. The short sword is best used indoors or in confined spaces or in close quarters with an opponent. The long sword is the most useful and versatile weapon you have; use it in any other situation.

On the battlefield, the bow is a little more advantageous than the *naginata*. With the bow you can take the offensive and strike from a distance, but the *naginata* is strictly a defensive weapon. All things being equal, the bow is superior to the *naginata*. They both have their strong points in confined spaces, but neither weapon is suitable for taking prisoners. They should both be kept on the battlefield, where they are essential.

On the battlefield, the bow is the most excellent tactical weapon for advance or retreat. It fires quickly and easily from between the ranks of other troops. It is an excellent weapon on the open battlefield. However, it is practically useless during sieges or when the opponent is more than forty yards away.

Remember, if you only practice in classrooms, you will lack proper focus and experience. You will get bogged down with rituals and petty details, and you will not serve well in real combat. Look around at all the martial-arts schools today, especially archery. There is far too much emphasis placed on ritual and appearance, and very little on reality. Archers from these schools are worthless in a fight.

Inside a fortress or on the open field before the troops clash, there is no weapon better than the gun, but once quarters are closed, the gun is inadequate. Even on the open field the bow has the advantage over a gun because you can see the path of the arrow and adjust your next shot; with the gun you cannot. Consider this carefully as you choose your weapons.

Your horse should be looked at as one of your greatest weapons. Your horse should be strong and fast and of good disposition and endurance. Your hand weapons should be strong also. Your swords should cut clean and deep. Your bow or *naginata* should be of the finest quality to pierce through armor. Both bows and guns should be well-built and accurate.

You should avoid becoming too dependent on any single weapon, or anything else really. Keep your options open and remain flexible. Too much dependence on any one thing is just as bad as not depending on anything. Never imitate others or rely too heavily on their advice. What works well for one may be disastrous for another. Use weapons that are most comfortable for you and feel good in your hands.

It is dangerous for leaders or troops to entertain likes or dislikes. Remain practical as you ponder these things.

TIMING

There is timing in everything under the sun. Understanding timing in strategy requires diligent practice and dedication.

In everything there is timing. It is easy to see timing in dance, music, horns, or stings because there is harmony and rhythm. However, timing is just as important in martial arts whether shooting a bow or a gun or riding a horse. You must recognize the timing and rhythm of all things.

There is also timing in emptiness.

There is timing throughout the life of a warrior. There is timing in your success and in your failures. There is timing in your gains and in your losses, in your promotions and in your demotions, in fulfillment and in disappointment.

In business, there are times of wealth and times of destitution. Business is like the waves of the sea. All things rise and all things fall. You must be able to discern the time you are in and the time that is approaching.

There are many different timings in strategy. The first thing you must learn is to differentiate between the proper time and the improper time for any action. You must know the proper amount of action and the speed with which to bring it about. Study distance and space and counterattack. These are essential principles of proper strategy. Unless you understand the timing of counterattack and reversal, your strategy will be weak and you will be in danger of being drawn into the timing of your opponent.

Strategic victory comes by knowing your opponent's timing and by attacking in a way that throws his timing off; using the timing of emptiness does this.

All five sections of my book are based on timing. You must train earnestly until you comprehend this timing. By training so diligently your understanding will develop and your spirit will grow strong.

My understanding of strategy is recorded for the first time by my own hand in these five sections called Earth, Water, Fire, Wind, and Emptiness. For those who wish to learn my strategy, you must follow this path:

1. Follow what is true and right, avoid dishonesty, and tell no lies.

2. Practice and train diligently.

3. Study every other art. You must be able to create beauty.

4. Learn the ways of all other professions.

5. Watch for the good and evil in all things.

6. Develop and trust your intuition.

7. Stay keenly aware of those things that you cannot see.

8. Study the details.

9. Avoid useless endeavors.

Embed these principles in your heart as you investigate the ideals of strategy. You must be able to see what is right in front of you and to pull back and see where it will lead you. Without this you cannot learn strategy. Once you have learned to do this you cannot be beaten even by twenty or thirty opponents. Above all, you must commit yourself to the study of strategy and train earnestly in the martial arts. When you can defeat people with your hands, you can defeat them with your mind or your eyes as well. With continued practice you can reach enlightenment, and once enlightened you can defeat ten men with your spirit alone. Even then, do not believe that you are invincible. No one is invincible.

Remember, large-scale strategy is based on picking the right people and proper personal conduct. In any field of endeavor, proper strategy knows how to avoid defeat, how to win over others, and how to live with honor.

The Book of Water

I named this section Water because water changes to adapt to its environment. Thus water is the inspiration for winning strategy. This idea of water is the very heart of my system of martial arts and the foundation of my strategy for the sword.

It is impossible to convey the full concept of the things I want to teach you through words. No form of communication can really pass this information on to you, but I believe, with proper practice, it will become self-evident. You should study each word in depth and concentrate on the details. If you think too generally you will miss the target.

I relay the lessons in here through concepts of individual duels, but understand that the same strategy applies to armies as well. You must open your thinking to grasp how this is so. Stand back and view the larger picture.

There is no room for error when your life is on the line, and if you miss the point even slightly at the beginning you will end up far from reality.

You will never master the principles of strategy simply by reading this book. You should read, study, and memorize the things written here and imitate the lessons, but even this alone will not bring enlightenment. You must absorb these things into your heart and seek your own path. After you have committed these lessons to your heart, you must learn from the inside out. Your own spirit will teach you. As understanding starts to break forth, grasp the concepts and ponder them deeply. You must exert yourself and constantly study very hard.

PROPER MENTAL ATTITUDE

For proper strategy, your mind should remain unchanged whether you are in the middle of a fight or resting and at peace. The mind should be unaffected by your circumstances. Carefully think this over. You should not be overly tense or overly relaxed. Your mind should remain open and clear, balanced and unbound. Do not let your thoughts stop on any one thing and you will react to everything. Free your mind from the burden of thought and even when you are asleep your mind will remain vigilant, and when you are rushed your mind will not be frantic. Your mind should not be encumbered with the burdens of the body, and your body should not be stressed by the thoughts of the mind. Let your mind lead, not your body. Let your mind be sharp and focused and do not be distracted by unimportant things. Do not think too highly of yourself and grow overconfident. Do not think too low of yourself and grow weak-hearted. Overconfidence and weak-hearted-ness are equally dangerous. Let your mind remain natural and your opponent will not read your intentions.

Your physical size is unimportant; keep your mind free from such traps. If you are small, remember, it is the power of your mind and of your sword that will cut down the giant. Therefore you are a giant. If you are large, do not rely on your strength; it is the power of your mind and sword that will kill your opponent, not your strength. Therefore you are small. You must not be bound by your size; too much confidence or too much fear are equally dangerous.

Keep your mind open and look at everything objectively. Study to sharpen your mind, and train to sharpen your spirit. Strive to improve your overall understanding and soon you will know good from evil. Learn from all paths and watch all people. Read past their actions and know their intentions and you will not be fooled by anyone. People's subtleties will become shockingly open to you and no one will deceive you. At this point you will know the power of martial arts. This is a special knowledge, and can be a heavy burden, but it is essential if you are to cultivate the arts of war and a steady mind.

STRATEGIC POSTURE

In attacking or defending, assume a stance with your head straight. Do not let your face tilt downward, skyward, or to the side. If your spirit is right your gaze will not wander. Your forehead will not be wrinkled, but your eyebrows will furrow. Do not blink; the first to blink is the one who will die. Narrow your eyes. Keep a calm expression, hold the tip of your nose straight, and thrust your chin forward. Flare your nostrils and keep your neck tense. From the shoulders down, every muscle should be equally tense. Keep your shoulders lower and your back straight, and do not let your buttocks poke out. Keep your knees pointed outward and grip the ground with your toes. Send power to your legs and tense your stomach so your hips stay straight. Tighten the knot of your hakama and wedge your short sword in at your side to tighten your waistband. Make sure that you are ready at all times. Your combat posture should be normal for you even in everyday life. Examine this carefully.

YOUR GAZE

You should concentrate your gaze broadly toward the center of the body. You should be able to see in two directions, both what you are looking at and the periphery. This way you will perceive the detailed movements as though you were standing back a few feet, and you will see the broader general movements in detail as though you were very close to them. In fighting with the sword, the movement of a foot or the tightening of a grip is vitally important. You must be able to take all of this in. Do not let your opponent distract you or "fake you out." Only intense training and experience will teach you to recognize the difference between what is important and what is meant to distract.

This is the same for individuals or for large armies in the middle of a war.

You must learn to take in everything without moving your eyes around or staring straight at your object. You will not learn to do this overnight; it will take time and training. Commit what I have written to memory and practice not focusing on any single part of your opponent. This will become your everyday way of seeing things.

YOUR GRIP

First, understand that when you take the sword in hand you do so with the resolve of killing. Your grip never changes from practice to combat. Grip lightly with the thumb and index finger, leave the middle finger neutral, and grip tightly with the ring finger and little finger. Leave no softness in your grip.

Draw your sword ready to take a life and you will not have to adjust your grip when you kill and your hand will not cringe. When you strike your opponent's sword, block, or pin his sword down, you should apply a little more pressure with your thumb and index finger.

Grip your sword the same way whether you are testing the blade or fighting for your life; there is no difference in grip.

Regardless of the weapon, avoid a rigid grip. A rigid hand clings to death. You should remain flexible, like a hand clinging to life.

YOUR FOOTWORK

Relax your toes and step firmly with your heels. Whether you move fast or slow, take large steps or small, you should move from stance to stance as comfortably as you walk down the street. I do not like the techniques for jumping or stances that are too light or too heavy.

You should move side to side with both feet. When you cut, block, or trap, you should set your feet deep for more power; this is done with both feet, not one. You should not favor one foot over the other for weight distribution.

THE FIVE GUARDS

There are only five guards: the upper, middle, lower, right side, and left side. There are no others. Since we call them guards it is easy to think of them as defensive, but you need to understand that they are offensive. They are used to put one into a position to take his life. Know them, be comfortable with them, and then forget them. The only thing that should be in your mind is the concept of killing your opponent.

Train your mind to take in the particulars of whatever situation you are in and use the most advantageous guard. The upper, middle, and lower guards will deliver more power for cutting, but the side guards are quicker and more fluid. Use the right or left guard in situations where there is no headroom or where one side is constricted. Pick the guard most suited to the situation.

Out of all the guards you should pay close attention to the middle guard as the best all-around guard. It offers every advantage that a guard can and has fewer disadvantages. Think of it this way—the middle guard is your command center and the other guards are there to protect it.

Spend as much time as you need to fully comprehend the guards.

THE WAY OF THE LONG SWORD

Enlightenment in the way of the long sword means you can wield it with no effort, even if you only use two fingers to hold it.

When cutting with the long sword, do not use quick, darting cuts. If you follow this way you will be in error and the long sword will be very hard for you the control. With the long sword you should follow through with your cuts in a fierce but controlled manner.

Do not try to use the long sword the way you might a folding fan or short sword. If you do, your cuts will not be right and the sword will be hard to handle. With the short sword you can use the short-sword chopping techniques, but with the long sword they will be weak and inefficient. You cannot kill a man by chopping at him with a long sword.

When you cut downward with the long sword, turn the blade and cut on the way back up also. When you cut from the side, turn the blade and cut on the return also. Let your elbows lead your cut and swing with power. This is the essence of cutting with the long sword.

Incorporate this with the five guards and soon you will handle the long sword naturally and easily, but it requires a lot of practice.

USING THE FIVE GUARDS: DRILLS

FIRST: THE MIDDLE GUARD DRILL

Assume the middle guard position, holding the tip of your long sword toward the opponent's face. When he cuts, parry the strike down and to the right. Hold your sword in place as a shield and he will have to bring his sword around for a downward cut. At this point, bring your sword back up and cut his arms from underneath.

This is the way I will show you how to use the five guards. You will not be able to learn any of them by simply reading. You must take the sword in hand and drill over and over. By repetitious use of these drills in the five guards you will come to know my techniques and strategy. There is no strategy for attacks other than the ones listed here, so you will know your opponent's techniques of attack also.

SECOND: THE UPPER GUARD DRILL

Take a guard in the upper position. As soon as you see your opponent's intent to cut you, strike. If the opponent avoids your cut, hold your sword where it is and wait for his strike. When he strikes, cut upward from below. Follow the same procedure if he avoids you again.

To properly use this technique you must properly time the opponent. There will be unique subtleties with every encounter. If you practice until you learn to do this from all five guards there will be no circumstances where you will not win. Practice, practice, and practice.

THIRD: THE LOWER GUARD DRILL

Take a lower guard position and wait for the opponent's strike. When he strikes, bring your sword up from below and cut his hands. One of two things will happen here: either you will make the cut and the opponent will be stunned or he will evade you and continue his strike. Stay in time with him and step quickly to the side; bring your sword over and cut his hands off.

The idea is to make this one continued movement starting from the lower position. This technique will work whether you cut with the first strike or not. The strategy of a continued strike is something you will see throughout your training. Everyone from the novice to the master uses this technique, so you should become very familiar with it.

FORTH: THE LEFT SIDE DRILL

Take a left-side guard with the sword pointing straight out from your side. When the opponent makes his cut, arc your sword down in a circular motion and cut upward; the hand should move from your shoulder toward your hip and cut the opponent's hand. Do this correctly and the opponent will be automatically blocked from his second strike.

FIFTH: THE RIGHT SIDE DRILL

Take a right-side guard with the sword pointing straight out from your side. As soon as the opponent commits to a strike, arc your sword to the rear and bring it directly overhead. Cut straight down with full force. Once you can effectively use this technique you will have complete control of the long sword.

That is enough on drills. These five are by no means exhaustive, but they will give you some ideas on using the long sword and help you to develop your timing and to read your opponent. Practice these drills daily to enhance your skills and your comfort with the long sword. In combat, it is essential to read the opponent's intentions, control the timing, and win by any means necessary. In the end, you or your opponent will die. You must resolve in your spirit that it will be the opponent, no matter what.

THE GUARD OF NO GUARD

The guard of no guard means that the long sword is not to remain in any fixed position. You should not insist on using any particular guard, but remain fluid and flexible. There are five guards from which to choose. You should use the one most appropriate for the situation. Observe the space, the opponent's guard, and the distance, and remember that the only point is to kill him.

You can shift from one guard to another very easily. From the lower guard you move the sword up a little and it becomes the middle guard. From the middle you move up a little more and it becomes the upper guard. The side guards are easily transitional as well, and you have a little latitude as to their exact position. Learn these transitions and you will have no fixed guard.

It is vitally important to have the proper frame of mind. When you take the sword in hand it is for one reason only; do not lay your hand to the sword lightheartedly. When facing an opponent, you should use every means to cut him down. A block is a strike and a strike is a block. If you parry, strike, hit, or even touch the opponent's sword, it is an opportunity for you to cut. Do not waste it. You must have this mindset, and if you think of anything else you will fail. You do not take the sword in hand to block, parry, or hit. You take it in hand only to kill.

This you must understand.

THE ONE-STRIKE KILL

Study timing and learn to kill the opponent in a single instant. Take a guard within sword's reach of the opponent and before he can decide on what to do, use the instant to strike down calmly and spontaneously. Strike as fast as possible with no concern as to the position of your body or stance. Cut with power.

This striking technique is known as the one-strike kill. Once you have the timing of this, use it with direct action and force. Go straight in and kill him. There is no other way. You either do it or you die.

THE TWO-STRIKE KILL

If you are ready to strike and you see the opponent is nervous and jumpy, fake the first strike. If the opponent jumps or flinches, wait for him to relax a bit and then kill him. As he lets himself relax his spirit will relax also and he will not be ready.

You cannot completely learn the timing of this technique from a book. You must practice. You must be able to see his reactions, receive this instruction, and seek understanding.

THE IMPULSIVE STRIKE

When you and the opponent square off and are both ready to attack, you should strike with everything within you. Strike with your body, your spirit, and from the mind of no mind, with extreme speed and power. This is known as impulse striking in perfect time without regard to form. This is the very essence of martial arts. Impulse strikes are very hard for some to understand, and even if they think they understand they may not. If you understand it you know it without a doubt. The only way to achieve this enlightenment is through continued study and practice.

THE FLOWING-WATER CUT

Use the flowing-water cut when you are in a clinch with an opponent who moves very quickly, blocks and parries very quickly, and springs very quickly. In a clinch he will try to jump back so he can spring forward with a new attack. At this point, feel the impulse and flash forward with your body, spirit, and emptiness. Match your timing to his movements like water matches the riverbed. Bring your sword around in an arc as though from behind and put it in the opponent with much power; lean into it with the weight of inactive water. Cut as slowly as you can to cut deeply and let his momentum work to your advantage.

Once you have mastered this timing it will be a very effective cut for you. You must be absolutely sure of your opponent's skill and positioning.

THE CONTINUOUS CUT

If the opponent tries to hook and parry your strike, continue the movement of your sword and cut at his head, arms, and legs without stopping the sword.

In one single, continuous movement, strike at him everywhere all at once. If he tries to hook and parry he is preparing to attack, and this cut will catch him off guard.

Once you have gained this skill, you will use it often. The only way to understanding here is detailed study and experience.

THE FIRE CUT

Use the fire cut just as you and your opponent's swords come into a clinch. Immediately drive forward with all of your force, mind, body, and spirit without repositioning your sword at all. As you come into a clinch or on-guard position, you may be able to collapse the opponent's guard and cut him. To do this you must act with shocking speed and force. This is a very useful technique once you have mastered it.

THE BLOOD-LEAF CUT

The idea of the blood-leaf cut is to take control of the opponent's sword by striking it.

When the opponent is waving his sword before you preparing to strike, parry, or trap, you strike his sword with the fire cut, but in the full spirit and power of the impulse cut. You should follow through and pin his sword down with your sword, pressing hard against his. If you do this properly you should force the opponent's sword from his hands.

The more you practice this the easier it will become to knock the opponent's sword from his hands. Practice with intensity.

THE LEADING-BODY CUT

Whenever you strike an opponent, you lead in with your body to create momentum and power then follow through with a full-power sword cut. Depending on the situation, there are times when the sword strikes independent of any body movement and times when the body strikes independent of the sword, but for the most part the body leads the sword. This technique is the foundation for your power. Practice it with every cut.

CHOP AND SLICE

Chopping and slicing are two separate things. To chop means you close in on the opponent with power of spirit, intending to kill him. Slicing is only cutting at the opponent over and over, usually to set him up for a killing chop.

Even if you slice with enough power to kill the opponent, it is still slicing. Chopping is always with the intent of killing or maiming.

In battle you may slice the opponent about the arms, legs, or torso in order to throw his timing off so that you can take his head with a chop. This is an astonishing technique when done properly. Learn it well.

THE SHORT-ARMED MONKEY CUT

By short-armed monkey I mean to teach you to keep your hands in close to your body for leverage and power. When you go in for the kill you should commit your whole being—body, spirit, and no mind—to the attack. If you reach out with your arms you naturally lean back and lose power, timing, and speed. When the opponent is about to strike and you charge in, it throws his timing off and gives you the advantage. Study this.

STICK LIKE GLUE

When you engage your opponent you should stick close to him. Do not become separated even a little or he will have the opportunity to cut you. Mold to his every move with your head, body, and legs.

Most people have a tendency to move in with their head and legs but keep their body back a bit. You must not let this happen.

HEIGHT

When you are facing an opponent, you should strive to be higher that him. Stretch your legs, body, and neck, but never cringe back. Stand tall in order to gain the advantage both in intimidation and in cutting power. Stand face to face with your opponent as if measuring your height against his. When you are taller, seize the opportunity and cut down with all your power.

You must be clever about this.

STICKY SWORDS

When you and an opponent are in close quarters with long swords, be determined to control the opponent's movements. You do this by sticking to his sword as he cuts. Intercept the sword in motion and affix your sword to it like glue. Being strong here does not mean striking with power. It means keeping contact with the opponent's sword so you can move, parry, or trap his blade.

There is a difference in sticking to his sword and becoming entangled. Entanglement is very dangerous, but sticking to his sword gives you the control.

You must learn the difference.

THE BODY STRIKE

The body strike is when you crash through the opponent's guard and slam into him with your full body weight. To do this best, turn your head slightly to the left, point your left shoulder at the opponent, and hunch down just a little. When you charge, slam your shoulder into his check while rising slightly. Charge in with full intensity and in time with your exhale.

Once you learn to do this right you may throw the opponent back eight or even twelve feet. When you have perfected this technique it is possible to kill the opponent with a body strike.

THREE BASIC PARRIES

There are three basic ways to parry an opponent's strike.

First, keep the tip of your sword pointed at his eyes or the center of his body and redirect his strike by moving your hand to the right.

Second, strike the opponent's sword back toward his own face by pushing your blade forward as though you were trying to take his head.

Third, take the short sword in your left hand and thrust your left hand toward the opponent's face. You catch his blade with your *tsuba* and push back, stabbing him in the face. Only at this point should you follow through with your long sword and kill him.

These are the three basic parries. You should think of the third as punching the opponent in the face with your left hand. Using the *tsuba* is a very precise move and requires diligent practice.

STAB AT THE FACE

Stabbing at the face is useful when you and the opponent are on guard with crossed swords and equal readiness. You lunge forward, driving the tip of your sword at his face. Drive forward as though your sole purpose is to stab his face. This will cause the opponent to shrink back with his face and his body. When the opponent shrinks back there are many opportunities presented to kill him.

In combat, if you cause the opponent to shrink back in body or especially in spirit, you have already won the fight; the only thing left is to take his life. Do not forget this technique.

Breaking the opponent's spirit is the highest form of martial arts. Practice with this in mind.

STAB AT THE HEART

Sometimes in fighting you will find yourself in an area where there is not enough room to swing your blade from overhead to the sides. In times like this you can stab straight at the opponent's heart.

This technique works well when you parry the opponent's thrust with the back of your blade and follow through with a thrust of your own. Point the tip of your sword at his chest and forcefully drive it directly into his heart without hesitation.

This technique is excellent to use when you are tired or if for any reason your sword will not cut well.

THE SPIRIT SHOUT

When you and the opponent attack with equal vigor, you may be able to gain the advantage by using a spirit shout. As you parry and ready to counterattack you can surprise your opponent with a loud spirit shout. The basic idea is to thrust the air upward from your abdomen with all the energy and force of your spirit and then cut the opponent down when he is shocked. This is not simply a loud noise; it is a force and a power. You can use the spirit shout when you are stabbing with the tip of the sword or when cutting with the edge.

You must use precise timing.

THE SLAPPING PARRY

In combat, when the opponent attacks and you touch swords, a slapping parry is very useful. Keep in mind that when using a slapping parry you are not really concerned with force. In fact, excessive force can be harmful. You are not attempting to catch or trap the opponent's sword either. You should use small circular motions to redirect his blade and follow up with an immediate attack, thus taking the offensive.

Once you have perfected this technique it does not matter how hard your opponent strikes; you will be able to deflect him with ease. When you use this technique you should have every intention of setting up your opponent for the kill.

This technique can only be learned by intense practice.

WHEN FIGHTING A MOB

This strategy is for an occasion when you may be surrounded by a mob. I find it best to draw both swords and hold them out to the left and to the right horizontal to the ground. Push the opponents in one direction regardless of the way they come in, even if from all sides at once.

Discern the opponents and kill the most aggressive first; kill the more timid later. Use your peripheral vision to see everything at once, and do not stare at anyone. Watch every movement, study the timing of the mob, and fight with both swords at the same time. Be very aggressive; waiting for them to attack is not good.

The strategy here is to remain ready with both swords out to the sides and kill the first one who comes into range; as he is falling, kill the next. Your spirit must be exceedingly strong to accomplish this. As the first few fall, chase the group into a bunch. You must be the aggressor here. You cannot afford to chase only the one who comes in on you. Do not accept the possibility that the mob can move you about; you must move them. It is essential to sense the mob's timing and know the weakest point to drive them.

Practice this with a group. Once you learn how to corner a mob, it is possible to take on twenty opponents at once and win.

THE ADVANTAGE

You can come to enlightenment through the study of the martial arts, but it can never really be explained in a book, so I will not try. The only way to enlightenment is through constant practice, study, and experience. This is why masters are masters, and beginners are beginners, and instructors are important.

DEATH BY A SINGLE BLOW

It is possible to kill an opponent with only one strike. No one can understand this without long study of the martial arts. If you practice until you gain this knowledge, you can strike opponents down at will, but it will only come by much training.

DIRECT INSTRUCTION

The best way to learn my strategy is though direct instruction. You must practice until this strategy becomes part of your soul, then you should pass it on to your own students.

The contents of the book of Water are an overview of the strategy of my teaching, written by my own hand. The way to learn martial arts is to start with basics and move to more advanced techniques. Practice the blocks and strikes until you gain total freedom of movement. Sharpen your mind and strengthen your fighting spirit. To really understand timing, you must face an opponent in battle where death or serious injuries are the only outcomes.

Once you have gained control of your body, fight from a non-stopping mind, and have beaten a few opponents, you will know the true way from the false. You should study everything that I have written here. Do not be impatient; a thousand-mile trek is conquered one step at a time. Absorb what is useful wherever you find it; reject what is bad. Never back down. Fight every time you get the chance with the mind of gaining strategic lessons.

Let your mind be free and remember that this is a lifelong study and a path that has no end. Make up your own mind to achieve more each day than you did the day before. Defeat weaker opponents today and you will kill fierce opponents tomorrow. Stay focused; do not let your-self become preoccupied.

No matter how many opponents you defeat, you must remain focused on the underlining strategy of each encounter and the teach-ings of this book. Once you reach enlightenment and free your mind, you will follow your instincts and defeat any number of opponents by yourself. Then you will come to understand large-scale strategy and military science.

This is the power of the martial arts. Study a thousand days to become proficient. Study ten thousand days to become enlightened.

The Book of Fire

In this book I liken my school of martial arts to fire. The matters of life and of death are written here.

Most people consider the study of martial arts a trivial thing and they make assumptions about it. Others study with a serious attitude, but they get wrapped up in small things like tiny movements of the wrist or fingers. Some devote the whole of their training to the study of only one thing, such as the fan or speed in the movements of the fore-arms. There are those who are concerned merely with speed, and they practice constantly with only a bamboo sword and never take steel in hand. Some devote themselves to the endless analyzing of leg and arm movements, searching for ways to be a little faster.

My way of strategy has withstood every form of combat where each time my life was on the line and I was faced with the option of killing or dying. This is how I learned martial arts. I have killed many opponents, both strong and weak, and I have learned where to find each man's weakness as well as his strength. I know how to use equally the cutting edge of the blade and the back ridge of the blade. I have been disciplined by blood and taught by the deaths of many opponents. Because of this, I do not concern myself with the pursuit of tiny, insignificant things. The true way of strategy is broad, not tiny. When you are faced with death you do not worry about the exact placement of your toes.

My martial-arts strategy was born in the deaths of those who came against me, whether it was one, five, or even ten at a time. The spirit is the power and the strategy works for either individuals or armies. Because of this you can learn the proper way to command armies from your one-on-one conflicts. If one man can beat ten, then a thousand men can beat ten thousand. Now, you cannot bring thousands of people together for daily practice, but you can come to the enlightenment of strategy by studying the people you face daily. For the most part, people are all the same. Armies of thousands follow the orders of a very few, or of only one, thus you are facing only one mind. Control your followers the same way. See them as extensions of your arms and legs and command them accordingly. This is why fighting one on one is the same as armies fighting armies. Understand a leader's strategy, his strengths, and his weaknesses, and you will know the strategy, strengths, and weaknesses of the ten thousand troops who follow him.

Enlightenment in my way of strategy will come to only a few of the most diligent students. In any path of study, only one in a thousand truly come to enlightenment. In strategy it is more like one in ten thousand. If you would be the one then you must be determined to achieve your goal at any cost. You must train without ceasing, day and night. You must forge your body and your mind in the fire of experience. You must polish your understanding in the light of truth. Truth is not what you want it to be; it is what it is, and you must bend to its power or live a lie. Free your mind from ego and thought. The time for thinking is when you are learning. Once you are enlightened, you act; you do not ponder endless scenarios. Develop your own intuition and trust your spirit. For any given situation there are many ways to survive, but there is only one best way, and your spirit will show it to you. Once you attain this level you will be in line with heaven and supernatural power will assist you to accomplish miracles. You must believe this.

YOUR ENVIRONMENT

Use the environment to give yourself the advantage in any situation. Follow basic principles, such as keeping the sun to your back so that it shines in your opponent's eyes. If you cannot position the sun to your back, keep it to your right side.

Indoors also, you should keep the light to your back or to your right side. You should make sure that there are no obstacles behind you and that you have sufficient room to your left so you can control the space to the right of you with the sword.

The same holds true at night. Take a position with the fire to your back and an opening to your right.

There is power in a higher position. Make sure that you are on higher ground than your opponent; even the slightest height advantage is valuable.

Remember, in fighting you should always chase your opponents to your left and then drive them into obstacles. Use your environment to trap him, and as soon as he is confused move in to kill. Do not give your opponent time to look around or consider his options. The same is true indoors. Drive him into corners, doorways, balconies, or furniture. Do not let up. Do not give him a chance.

In any given situation you should control the opponent by driving him to a place of imbalance. Drive him into narrow places to obstruct his movement. Use everything in the immediate area to your advantage. Take control and kill.

You must study this thoroughly and practice diligently.

THE THREE ENGAGEMENTS

There are only three ways to engage the opponent.

1. You attack the opponent suddenly and immediately without giving any indication beforehand.

2. You bait the opponent into attacking and immediately kill him with a strong counterattack.

3. You and the opponent both attack suddenly without warning.

These three are known as Ken no Sen, Tai no Sen, and Taitai no Sen, respectively. These are the only three ways of engagement, and there are no others.

This strategy is known as the strategy of the first strike, and you can win quickly if you understand it. Knowledge of the first-strike principle is of primary importance in martial arts. There are many variations and aspects to the concept of first-strike strategy, and it is useless to try and explain it fully since every encounter will have its unique circumstances. Winning by first-strike strategy is achieved by accurately reading the intentions of your opponent. A few can do this, but most cannot, and that is why only a few become masters. The technique requires keen insight and a solid trust of your intuition.

KEN NO SEN—THE FIRST ATTACK

To successfully use the first attack, you should remain very calm both inside and out. Take a relaxed position facing the opponent and then suddenly, from nowhere, explode into the attack with all of your force and power of spirit. Remember that it is wise to leave a little reserve for a second attack. The onset should be shocking and overwhelmingly forceful.

Let go of your thoughts and let your spirit direct you. Set your mind at ease and do not think about how to attack, just attack with the spirit of terror and death. In the span of a single breath, crush your opponent's courage and cause him to tremble. Resolve your heart to win under any circumstances and do not stop until the opponent is lying dead at your feet.

TAI NO SEN—THE SECOND ATTACK

There are two ways to use this attack.

First, wait for your opponent to attack and then feign weakness to bait him. When he attacks, jump back as though you are afraid. When you see his intensity fade, rush in forcefully and kill him.

Second, wait for the opponent to charge in with force, then immediately charge in more aggressively than him. When you see he has lost his timing, crash through his guard and kill him.

These are the two ways of Tai no Sen.

TAITAI NO SEN—THE THIRD ATTACK

Use the third attack when the opponent charges in fiercely. You should remain calm, yet strong, and when the opponent is within range, sharpen your spirit and rush him, then overpower and kill him. If the opponent comes in quietly and carefully, you should rush in quickly to throw off his timing. Fake a technique and watch his reaction. If he is thrown by it, take the advantage and kill him.

This is Taitai no Sen. It is impossible to explain any better than this, but you should be able to gain enlightenment with your insight. You should not always be the one who is attacking, even though it is usually better to take the lead and put the opponent on the defensive. Either way, you will win if you study these things I have written and commit them to heart.

HOLDING DOWN A PILLOW

By holding down a pillow I mean not letting the opponent raise his head. In fighting and in martial arts, it is bad to be lead around by the opponent or to stay on the defensive. You must be determined to lead the opponent around regardless of anything else; he must be the one on the defensive.

Now, it is obvious that the opponent will think the same as you and try to take the offensive. Use this knowledge and the manner in which he attacks. Stop him when he tries to attack. Prevent him when he tries to jump. Control him when he tries to grapple. To successfully use this strategy in the heat of combat you must trust your intuition and know what the opponent intends to do given even the slightest clue. Perceive his intentions and stop him before every move. Stop his attack at the letter a. If he is about to strike, stop him at the s. If he is about to jump, stop him at the j, and if he wants to cut, stop him at the c.

It is important to let the opponent expend his energy on anything useless, but you should stop him from doing anything that might give him the slightest advantage. Let him work to set up his strategy, and then cut him short of fulfilling his plan.

With this strategy you cannot wait to see the opponent's plan taking shape. You must comprehend it at the very thought then lead him along the path to his own death. To control the opponent by his own thought process is the very heart of strategy. When you can do this you are a master, and will understand anything you set your mind to.

CROSSING A SEA

When I speak of crossing a sea I am talking of both a body of water and various situations in your life. Be it a hundred miles of choppy water or a turbulent time in your life, the spirit of the conqueror is the same. There come many times in life when a person must set sail and chart out his own path, even if his companions remain safely ashore.

At this time you should learn your route, know your vessel, and watch for the best season. Learn the dangers and face the fears. Ride the wind as long as you can, but if the wind stops and conditions become unfavorable, be ready to take the ore in hand and force your way to the port.

To be successful in life one must have the same spirit. Many obstacles will arise and many opponents will come against you, but do not be detoured. Make up your mind, be decisive, trust your intuition, and follow your spirit. Trust the experience of others, but do not let them cause you to doubt your intuition.

In martial arts and in strategy, this analogy is important. Know your opponent like a sea captain knows the ford. Learn his strengths and his weaknesses. Know the best plan of attack and never relent. Do not be distracted. Do not be dissuaded. Have a resolute spirit in everything you do.

Attack the opponent's weak points. Always seek the position of advantage and never stop until you win. Once you have achieved your goal you may rest.

DISCERNING THE SITUATION

In combat, both large scale and individual, you must learn to discern the opponent's situation. What is his character? Is his fighting spirit strong or weak? What is the condition of the battlefield?

Once you know these things you can move your troops around, gain the position of advantage, and take the victory. Comprehend his strategy and fight the battle with the foreknowledge of his plan.

In one-on-one combat it is also necessary to discern the opponent's disposition. Gauge his fighting spirit, his strengths and weaknesses, and his expectations. Perceive his timing and attack in surprising ways. If your intuition is sharp you will know the opponent's secrets and nothing can be hidden from you. Once this understanding becomes part of you, you will find many ways to destroy opponents.

You must fully develop and then trust your intuition.

TRAMPLE THE OPPONENT

Trampling the opponent is used in every facet of martial arts. It is even used in large-scale military operations, especially if the opponent is armed with bows or guns. The idea is not to let them get a second shot. After they have fired their first volley you must overrun them as they reload for the second round. If you do not you will simply sit there and die. You must charge up your spirit and attack the opponent with force.

In one-on-one combat, if you strike with your sword only after your opponent's strike you will spend your time on the defensive and you will get nowhere. Once the opponent strikes you must run over him, trample him, and stop him from making a second strike. You must control the opponent or he will control you.

In either context, trampling the opponent is not with your feet only. You must trample him with your spirit, your body, and your weapon. You must overpower him with your whole being and take the offense. Once on the offense, do not settle with simply cutting him down; you must control him in every way.

This will require more study.

UNDERSTANDING COLLAPSE

Everything that you know in life has one inevitable end. Everything will collapse. Houses collapse. Structures collapse. Societies collapse. And even your opponent will collapse. Everything collapses when its time runs out.

In large-scale military operations, it is important to chase the opponent down when he has broken his timing so as to take the advantage. If you do not take advantage of the opponent's misstep, he may recover and kill you.

In one-on-one combat there are times when the opponent's timing will be out of sync and his momentum starts to collapse. It is vitally important to follow up on any little mistake that your opponent makes to keep him from regaining the advantage. Never underestimate the ability of your opponent to recover. You must watch carefully for the opponent's misstep and charge him when you see it and take his life. The time to strike is when the opportunity presents itself.

You must be direct and powerful and strike with speed and death.

BECOME THE OPPONENT

To become the opponent means to take on the opponent's frame of mind and to put yourself in his situation.

There is always more than one way to consider. Take a robber who is caught in the act. He draws his weapons and barricades himself in the house while people gather outside. To the untrained person on the outside, the robber appears to be a fortified and powerful opponent, but the robber sees himself as trapped with nowhere to run and the whole world against him. If the robber follows this line of thought he will take on the attitude of a pheasant. The one going in after him should take on the attitude of a hawk. In any engagement, the ultimate winner will always be the one with the spirit of a hawk. Concentrate on this.

In large-scale military operations as well, people tend to think of the opponent as fearsome. This can cause you to take a weak or passive stance. If you have a strong military, good troops, and a solid strategy, do not worry about the opponent. You simply cannot sit around afraid of what the opponent might do.

The same holds true for your individual conflicts. If you face an opponent with the thought that he is a master technician and strategist, then you have already lost. Be the hawk, not the pheasant. Never accept an inferior position to anyone. It is the strongest spirit that wins, not the most expensive sword.

RELEASE FOUR HANDS

The idea of the four hands is for when you and the opponent are equally matched in technique and strategy. The idea is four hands attached to the same body and controlled by the same mind so that you and your opponent counter each other on every move. If you find yourself in a deadlock such as this you must immediately change strategy. Do something to surprise the opponent and throw him off guard, and then strike him down.

In large-scale military operations, when you come to this impasse and are deadlocked so that you can't gain the advantage, you must release the four hands and strike with something new. The longer you wait to change strategy, the more of your people will die for nothing. As soon as you recognize a deadlock, you must immediately abandon your old plan of attack and come up with something that will take the opponent off guard.

In the heat of individual combat you will at times face the same situation. You must be able to immediately size up the opponent's situation and attack in a new way.

MOVE THE SHADOW

At times you may find yourself against an opponent who is difficult to read with certainty, or who is hard to discern. The technique for feeling out the opponent is known as moving the shadows.

In large-scale military operations, it is sometimes difficult to know the attitude of your opponent. In this case, you fake a powerful attack and watch his reaction. He will show you his attitude and you will know how to plan your strategy in order to take advantage of this knowledge and win.

In individual combat, if the opponent takes a guard with his sword behind him or to his side so that you cannot tell what he is planning, you should fake a cut with enough force to cause him to react. Then you will know his strategy. You should follow up quickly and cut him down. If you wait too long to attack, the opponent might realize that he has given away his strategy and change his plans. Seize the opportunity and kill him. You must be diligent.

ATTRACT THE SHADOW

Attracting the shadow is for a time when you can clearly see the opponent's attitude and plan of attack.

In large-scale military operations, you will sometimes know what the opponent is up to and what he is planning. This is a huge advantage and assures victory, but if you are too quick to react to his moves he will stop and change his plan and you will lose the advantage and possibly the victory. Wait, draw back, and let your opponent move forward with his plan until you have him where you want him. Create an attractive situation for him, and then use it to kill him.

In individual combat there will also be times when you can read the opponent's strategy by following his timing and rhythm. Use this knowledge. Wait for the right opportunity and kill him. Do not let him think that you have his timing or he may change suddenly and cut you down.

INFECT THE OPPONENT

Look around at all the things that can be infectious. Sleepiness can be infectious. Yawning can be infectious. Timing and rhythm can also be infectious.

In large-scale military operations, the opponent at times may seem rushed and under pressure to attack quickly. In these times you should display a relaxed, laid-back attitude and you will see the opponent start to relax in kind. Lull them into this state, then charge up your spirit and attack with speed and power.

This strategy works well also in individual combat. When the opponent is fierce and his spirit is high, you should appear to relax a bit. You will usually see the opponent relax a bit also. That is when you take his life.

Another technique is called intoxication and is similar to infection. Through method you can pass on to the opponent boredom, restlessness, anger, or fear. You should study each of these separately.

IMBALANCE

In all things there is balance and imbalance, harmony and discord. Use this knowledge to throw your opponent's timing or balance off. There are several ways to do this:

1. Cause him to feel that death is closing in on him.

2. Make him feel that his situation is hopeless.

3. Surprise him with the unexpected.

You must thoroughly research these strategies.

In large-scale military operations it is wise to bring about your opponent's imbalance. One way to do this is to attack unexpectedly with brutal power and fortitude, then stop just short of engagement. As the opponent drops his guard, rush in and kill him. Keep the opponent unsettled in such ways and your victory is at hand.

In individual combat it is possible to win victory in the same way. Close in on the opponent slowly and without intensity then suddenly and quickly take his head. You cannot give the opponent even one breath to catch on to you. You must kill him in a single instant.

FEAR

Fear is a common thing. Surprise or the unknown often causes it. You can use fear to your advantage.

In large-scale military operations more than just what the opponent sees can frighten him. You can frighten him with your shouts or by appearing larger and stronger than him or by surprise attacks from out of nowhere. All of these cause fear, and if you use them properly and know when to seize the opportunity, you can destroy your opponent.

In individual combat you should use fear to gain victory. Frighten the opponent with your body, your weapons, or your voice. Most importantly, you should frighten him with your spirit. Startle the opponent by doing something unexpected and powerful. Take advantage of his twitch to kill him.

Pay close attention and learn to read your opponent.

BLENDING

Blending is used when you and an opponent are engaged in head-to-head battle, force against force, and you cannot gain the advantage.

Blending with the opponent is to continue the struggle as before, then suddenly shift and take advantage of his power to throw him off balance. If he pushes and you push back equally neither of you will move, but if you suddenly move back, he will fall forward. This is what blending with the opponent's strength and timing is.

In large-scale military operations the same technique can be used. If you and an opponent are squared off and you cannot overpower him, let him push through and trap him. Use the opponent's strength to win over him.

ATTACK THE EDGES

There will be times when you are up against a strong or very skilled opponent and a head-on attack will not give you an advantage. In this case you attack the edges.

In large-scale military operations it is useful to study the strengths of the opponent and attack the weak areas. If you cannot attack his command center, attack his outposts. Chip away at his edges and you will soon weaken the whole of his operation. Once he is weakened it is wise to continue the attack at the edges until they completely collapse. You can then work your way to the heart.

In individual combat it is the same. If you cannot cut his throat, then cut his hand. If you cannot cut his hand, then cut his fingers. Nick away at him until he is in pain and weak, and victory will be easily had.

CONFUSION

Confusion means keeping the opponent guessing as to what you are about to do.

In large-scale military operations it is important for you to keep the opponent guessing. Use your strategy and any techniques you can think of to keep him wondering—if you are going here or there, fast or slow, now or later. Use this strategy to fluster the opponent and then, when the timing is right, move straight in and kill him immediately.

In individual combat use this same strategy to fake the opponent out and keep him guessing. Start one technique, but finish with another. Make it look like you are charging in, and then don't. Make it look like you are standing guard, and then attack. Confuse him until the right moment then rush in and strike him down.

THREE KIAI, OR SHOUTS

Shouting is a technique that can be very useful in many different situations. There are basically three types of shouts: the beginning shout, the during shout, and the final shout. The shout should be in accord with the situation. We use the shout to work up our spirit in emergencies such as fires or tidal waves and storms.

In large-scale military operations, the shout running into battle is loud and frightening in order to drive up your fighting spirit and intimidate your opponent. During battle, the shout is individual and lower. At the conclusion, the shout is high-pitched and celebratory in revelry of victory.

In individual combat you can also use the kiai just before dealing the deathblow to unsettle the opponent. You lash out instantly after the shout. After the opponent is defeated it is customary to give a victory shout. These are the before and after shouts.

You should not shout at the same instant you strike—remember, they are used to set the opponent up for the strike. Also, use the kiai to maintain the control and rhythm and timing of the situation.

FUSING

In large-scale military operations, fusing is where you face a stronger opponent and you concentrate the brunt of your strike at his strong point. Hit him hard, and as soon as you see him pull back a little, immediately strike another strong point. Basically, you should attack in a zigzagging manner.

This technique is also valuable when you are alone fighting a mob. Attack the strongest first, and as soon as you have killed him or driven him off attack the second-strongest opponent, and so on. Your body movements will be side to side and zigzagged in time with the mob.

Read your opponent well and attack with resolute determination not to back away until he is destroyed. Fusing is to attack the opponent with the spirit of kill or die, and to remain strong until your opponent is dead.

CRUSHING

To use the crushing technique you must charge up your fighting spirit and view the opponent as weak and feeble then charge in and crush the life from him in one strike.

In large-scale military operations, you should view your opponent as small in number even if he is large. You posture yourself like a giant and take to the battlefield accordingly. Your opponent will see this and lose heart, and that's when you destroy him. You must attack with the mind of grinding him to powder. If you attack weakly he may recover and kill you. Think of crushing as completely grinding some small thing in the grip of your fist.

In individual combat when your opponent is not overly skilled, has a weak fighting spirit, has poor timing, or is afraid and about to run back, it is important for you to seize the opportunity and attack him. Do not let that moment pass or he may grow stronger. Attack and kill him in the span of one breath or the blink of an eye.

THE MOUNTAIN AND THE SEA

In combat it is very dangerous to repeat the same attack too often. Sometimes you will have no choice but to use the same tactic a second time, but never use it a third. If you are unsuccessful with a particular technique once, it is very unlikely that it will work the second time around, and the third time it could get you killed.

After the second attempt you must find a different technique and then launch your next attack completely differently. Try to surprise him and you may find victory.

If the opponent stands like a mountain, you should move like the sea. If he moves like the sea, you should stand like a mountain. This is the idea of the mountain and the sea strategy.

BREAK THE SPIRIT

In combat it is possible to appear victorious on the surface but still not win. If you leave your opponent with any fighting spirit he will not accept defeat and will still be a danger to you. You must completely break his fighting spirit.

In this case, you charge up your spirit and change your strategy to force the opponent to acknowledge utter defeat from the bottom of his soul. You have no choice; he must acknowledge defeat in his heart or he must die.

This is breaking the spirit and it is accomplished with the sword, the body, and most of all, with your spirit. The spirit is the warrior. It can be difficult to know for sure that you have broken his spirit, but if you do you can let him live and no longer worry about him. If you cannot completely break his spirit, you must kill him. If you leave an opponent alive with even a small amount of fighting spirit, he will be very dangerous.

REJUVENATION

Rejuvenation occurs when you are in a deadlock with an opponent and can make no headway. When this happens you should shake off your old attitude and begin all over with a new spirit and attitude. Pick up a new timing and think in a new way. Then you may be able to find the key to victory.

Anytime you find yourself in difficult circumstances you should use rejuvenation. Sometime circumstances are impossible to change, but your attitude is easily changed. Once you have a different attitude, find another way to win.

This is even important in large-scale military operations. Masters of strategy understand this.

RAT'S HEAD, OX'S NECK
SMALL AND LARGE

When you find yourself deadlocked with an opponent over small details, suddenly switch your view to the large picture. Instead of worrying over tiny details, concentrate on the overall strategy. Leave the opponent to worry about the tiny things. Step back and find another way to win.

The warrior should live by this rule both day and night and never conduct any affair without this understanding.

COMMAND THE OPPONENT

Having aspired to the mastery of strategy, a general knows his troops. Use the knowledge of command to take charge of the opponent or the opponent's troops. Take on the spirit of his commander and you can move him about at will.

LET GO THE HILT

This has a number of meanings. It means winning without a sword, and it means losing with a sword in hand. Let go the hilt means you should take on the spirit to win whether you have a weapon or not.

BODY LIKE A ROCK

Train so that your technique and strategy are as solid as a large rock. Once you achieve this no one will disturb you or cause you alarm.

This I will teach you in person.

The things written above are the things that seem to have occurred over and over throughout my lifetime study of martial arts. This is the first time I have taken brush in hand to try and write them out, so they seem a little out of order to me, and some of them are very hard to properly explain on paper. But in any case, this is a necessary starting point for anyone wanting to learn strategy.

This is something I have studied since childhood, and I have forged my spirit and my technique in battle and in every kind of situation. In contrast, I have seen many supposed masters and listened to them chatter about this and that and watched their technique. For the most part they are all liars and showoffs with no real knowledge of martial arts. They train only to attract attention and do not know the true way.

Some of them really believe what they are saying because they have never tested it. These are the parasites that feed off of the truth and only serve to destroy that which they claim to treasure. There are many of these, and they will be the ultimate corruption of the true way.

The true way of martial arts is to fight real battles of life and death. There are no substitutes. Train hard. Fight hard. Study hard. Practice everything just as I have written here and you will attain enlightenment, and then you will never be defeated.

The Book of Wind

If you expect to fully comprehend my teaching on strategy it is necessary to compare and contrast it against other schools of thought. In this Book of Wind I shall write about them at some length. Some of these rely heavily on using extra-long swords, and some concentrate only on power. Others use only the shorter long sword, and still others teach an endless list of techniques and focus on internal power.

In this book I will expose those teachings for what they really are, and I will show you the difference between the true way and the path of lies. My teachings on strategy stand apart from all others in that they were born in blood. The others mostly dress up strange and silly techniques to sell, as one would arrange flowers or paint teacups for the market.

Most people view martial arts from a very limited standpoint and see martial-arts training as a way of fighting only. Do not be deceived—martial arts is much more than simply training in fighting techniques. In fact, the physical aspect is the least of the goals. Those who view martial arts this way are far from enlightenment.

I will attempt to point out the errors made by most schools, one by one. You should study these diligently until you can see the errors yourself and by this you will understand the true path of my strategy.

EXTRA-LONG SWORDS

There are schools out there that rely on an extra-long sword. In my way of thinking, this is a weakness. These people rely on the length of their weapons because they do not understand the basic principles of strategy, which is mainly the idea of winning by any means necessary. They see the length of their blade as an advantage because they think it will allow them to kill the opponent from a distance.

These people say things like, "Even an extra inch of reach is vital," but they say things like this because they have no real knowledge of strategy. If anything, their reliance on an extra-long sword proves they have no heart for fighting and a weak and feeble spirit. Their only strategy is to get as far away from the opponent as possible. The long sword itself can be very disadvantageous if you are faced with an opponent who closes the gap with a short sword. The long sword then becomes very difficult to wield.

Of course, they have their own reasons for using the extra-long sword, but they are not realistic. Their reasoning only stands up in theory, but in actual combat they would die quickly. Wordy arguments may sound reasonable, but in the light of truth they fade away.

Does a warrior using a regular long sword always lose to a warrior using an extra long sword?

Consider also the circumstances where you may have limited room overhead or to the sides. In these cases, the extra-long sword is practically useless whereas the shorter sword is still useable. Remember, you cannot always choose where you will fight, so insistence on an extra-long sword is a departure from the true spirit of strategy. Also, using an extra-long sword requires more strength and stamina; some have this, but many do not.

There is an old saying: "Great and small go hand in hand." This is a true saying, so remember it. You should not hate the long sword, but you should not become too dependent on it either. As for myself, I do not hate the extra-long sword; what I hate is the attitude of insistence on it.

In large-scale military operations, the extra-long sword can be compared to a very large body of troops, and a smaller sword to a smaller body of troops. Can a smaller force do battle with and even overcome a larger force? Of course. History has many examples of this.

In my strategy, we do not dislike the extra-long sword, or any weapon for that matter. As for my followers and myself, we do not entertain narrow-minded or preconceived attitudes. Martial arts are alive and fluid, and you must have the mind to take all things into account.

OVEREMPHASIS ON POWER

You should not fall into the trap of believing in a strong long sword or a weak long sword. Overuse of power is not a good thing. If you cut with the mind of being very strong, your cut will be crude and sloppy. It is almost impossible to consistently win by relying on strength alone.

Also, if you attack an opponent with the mind of cutting him down by reason of a very powerful cut, it is quite possible that you will miss him entirely and endanger yourself. It is important to resist the temptation to cut with extra force even when test-cutting.

When you are in a battle for your life, your objective is to kill the opponent. Free your mind from all considerations of power or speed and simply kill the opponent. Close in with that one intention and let your sword follow its own path.

If you are in the habit of cutting with extra force, you will find a time when you hit the opponent's sword too hard and it will cause your own sword to deflect; then you will lose your timing and balance and maybe even your head.

In large-scale military operations, if you strive for strength by building a very large force then your opponent will also build a very large force and you will gain little. The true key to victory is proper planning and strategy. If strategy calls for a large force, you should use a large force, but if strategy calls for a smaller force then you should use a smaller force.

Do not get caught up in trifles or senseless plotting. Dismiss that which is impossible and search for that which is advantageous. Be crafty and wise. Win by any means necessary.

USING A SHORTER LONG SWORD

To depend on the use of a shorter long sword for victory is not the way of true strategy. Since long ago, warriors have used a long sword and a short sword. By training hard, a person can make himself more powerful and wield the long sword comfortably, so why bother with a medium-sized one?

Those who use a medium-sized sword believe they have an advantage against long-range weapons, such as the spear or the *naginata*. They think they can jump in between the strokes of the longer weapon and catch the opponent unprepared. This is a false view and it is not good strategy.

The idea of trying to time an opponent's strokes in order to move in between them is foolish, and it causes you to leave other areas open for attack or to miss opportunities to kill the opponent. Also, this idea is not useful when there is more than one opponent.

The idea that a medium-sized sword allows you more dexterity so that you can jump about and twirl while cutting in all directions is silly. The fact is that you would spend all of your energy on defense trying to block the attacks of an opponent with a regular long sword. This is not good strategy. You should charge straight at your opponents with your body and your spirit strong, causing them to scatter. Leap at them and cause them to doubt their resolve.

In large-scale military operations, all things being equal, it is better to gather a larger force and attack the opponent when he least expects it. Attack fiercely and crush all resistance.

People of the world ordinarily practice martial arts by parrying, dodging, and evading. This becomes the foundation on which they build their strategy, and they are easily led around because of it. The proper way of martial arts is to charge straight to the heart and kill the opponent in one breath. It is vitally important to develop a strong fighting spirit and the right attitude toward killing.

Think this over carefully.

EMPHASIS ON NUMEROUS TECHNIQUES

When I see a school that teaches a large variety of cutting techniques, I know right away that it is not a school of real fighting strategy. These people spend their time practicing many techniques to impress the gullible students who pay them for lessons. This frame of mind is vile and should be repulsive to the true warrior.

There are only so many ways to kill with the sword, and to argue on and on otherwise is foolish. You take the sword in hand and you cut the opponent down. You either do this or you don't do it. There is no middle ground. This is the same for the master warrior as it is for women and children. Anyone who was ever killed by the sword was killed by a thrust or a cut. There is no other way.

Given that there are only two ways to kill with a sword, I fail to see the reason for practicing hundreds of little tricks to do it. It is better to be the master of a few techniques than it is to be feeble with many.

In my experience, you need no more than five cutting or thrusting techniques, and you should be able to do them from any of the five positions in case you are in an area with obstructions overhead or to the sides.

Practicing silly things like twisting the hands for more power, twirling around, or jumping about, is a waste of time and may get you killed in real combat. To kill someone you go straight in and kill them; there is no need for foolish antics. If anyone should twirl or jump about it should be the opponent's spirit. You should stand tall and your spirit should be direct and foreboding.

OVEREMPHASIS ON THE GUARD

You are mistaken if you spend too much time worrying about your guard position and if you spend all of your time perfecting a guard in a classroom against no opponent. This causes people to study too deeply into theory and compels them to try and improve the older ways with newer, more modern ways.

The truth is that victory comes only by manipulating the circumstances to your advantage while disrupting your opponent's timing. This has always been true, and no amount of thinking will change it.

When you take a guard you can no longer change and manipulate circumstances. You have simply to stand by and wait for the opponent to make the first move. This is bad. It places you on the defensive and you are left with nothing to do but react to your opponent.

In large-scale military operations, the guard refers to a fort or some immovable force that you must make unassailable. But even here, victory comes by timing the opponent and launching into an offensive strike at the appropriate moment. In either case, it is deadly to take a strong guard and wait for the opponent to make the first move. Think this over carefully.

I do not like the stationary and defensive nature of taking a guard. In my experience, you must charge the opponent. You need to upset him, anger him, or terrify him into breaking his timing or to break his fighting spirit. You cannot do this standing still. That is why I teach you to take a guard without taking a guard and to defend without being defensive. Every guard and every defense should be an offensive technique.

In large-scale military operations you should size up your opponent and make the best use of the conditions of the battlefield. You should insure that your own troops are well-supplied, charge up their fighting spirits at the right time, and then strike the opponent with force and resolve.

You will have a completely different attitude if you launch the first attack than you would if you were fending off the opponent. With a spirit of defensive guard, you might as well take your spears and *naginatas* and build fences with them to try and keep the opponent at bay. If you are interested in attacking you should have the spirit to take fence polls and railings and use them as spears and *naginatas* to kill the opponent.

THE GAZE

Different people will answer the question differently as to where you should affix your gaze while in combat. There is no consensus or generally agreed-upon method. Some want to concentrate on the opponent's long sword, others on the opponent's hands. There are those who teach that you should concentrate on the feet or the face of the opponent. The truth is that if you concentrate on any single thing you will be easily distracted and drawn into the opponent's timing.

Take football players, for example. They can move the ball about, kick it, catch it, and complete every sort of complicated task without staring at it or taking their general gaze off their opponents. The players have become accustomed to the ball and no longer have to concern themselves with it. A juggler can balance a door on the tip of his nose while juggling several sharp swords in the air at the same time, all without concentrating his gaze on any single thing.

The same is true of battle. A warrior should be able to see the whole of the opponent without looking right at him. Use your peripheral vision and you can follow the movements of his sword, hands, feet, and head at the same time. You concentrate your gaze at the void and concentrate your spirit to reading his spirit.

In large-scale military operations, it is also important not to concentrate on any one thing. Keep your gaze broad and take in the whole of the opponent at once. Let your spirit read the spirit of the opponent's entire army as though you were reading a single opponent. There is a difference between seeing and perceiving. In seeing, you can only take in what is there to be seen. In perceiving, you can read your opponent's very heart and mind. By seeing, you can tell where the opponent is. By perceiving, you can tell where he is going. Perceive the opponent's situation, his readiness for battle, and the state of his troops, and attack at the most advantageous time to ensure victory.

Whether in single combat or large-scale military operations, there should not be a narrow focus. You must open your mind to perceive all things and react accordingly. Do away with all preconceived ideas and move in accordance with the timing of the situation. Narrow-minded people lose focus quickly because they cannot comprehend anything outside of their limited experience. They are easily distracted and easily killed. Strive to remain open to every aspect of every situation. Force your mind to accept unreasonable possibilities and you will become invincible.

FOOTWORK

In the world of martial arts there are many methods of footwork taught. There is the floating step, the jumping step, the springing step, the stomping step, and so on. I do not believe any of these give an advantage.

I do not like the floating step because it teaches you to be light on your feet, and you need to be solid on your feet when you strike.

I do not like the jumping step because it causes you to become jumpy and it is a bad habit.

I do not like the springing step because it is detrimental to be leaping all over the place. The stomping step puts you on the defensive, and I particularly dislike it. I do not like quickstepping techniques, such as the crow step, either.

In fighting, you never know if you are going to engage the opponent in the marsh, on rocky ground, on a hill, or even in a stream or confined place. For this reason, I do not like practicing techniques of footwork as though there were one to fit every situation.

In my way of thinking you should fight in the manner most natural to you. I move about in combat the same as I do walking down the street. I tailor my footwork to the timing of the opponent on the spot;

I move fast or slow when necessary and never concern myself with the tedious details of stepping methods.

In large-scale military operations, footwork is also important. You should not set your mind on any particular way of movement or you will not be as quick to adapt to the opponent. If you charge in with preconceived ideas you will not be open to reading the opponent and may let the opportunity to win pass you by without even seeing it.

In either large-scale military operations or in individual combat, it is imperative to watch the opponent's spirit. Read when he is tired, confused, or off-balance, and use that knowledge to kill him.

OVEREMPHASIS ON SPEED

Speed in martial arts is not the true way of strategy. In reality, speed or slowness is only that which is out of time with the situation. The proper speed at which to execute a technique should flow of its own accord. You should always strive to free your mind so the sword can follow its own path, and if you are concentrating on speed this is impossible.

The sword master can place his strike at a student's neck before the student even has time to react; yet the master never appears to speed or hurry his sword along. In fact, the master appears very relaxed and unconcerned. An experienced courier can run many miles at a time, but he does not try to run at the fastest speed all day long. The novice runner can run his fastest all day long and not cover the same ground as an experienced runner who appears to take his time. The same applies to music. The best drummer beats the drum in time with the music. If the melody is fast the drummer is fast, and if the melody is slow the drummer is slow. It would not do for the drummer to beat the drum out of time whether faster or slower.

Indeed, experts from any field make their work appear relaxed and not hurried. They have quit trying to do the thing and now they simply do it.

To concentrate on speed is even worse in martial arts than in other areas. You should always follow the timing of the situation and never rush it. Overdependence on speed is not a good thing. If you move too fast and are out of sync with your opponent, your blade will not be where it is supposed to be and you will die.

In large-scale military operations, it is very dangerous to follow a hurried spirit. You must time your moves well and follow the spirit of good timing. Using the technique of holding down a pillow will keep you in good time, neither too fast nor too slow.

Strive to remain calm and steady even in a crowd of people rushing here and there. You are a warrior. You should lead those that are less settled, not follow them. This state of mind will only come with practice and time.

THE FOUNDATION AND THE ENLIGHTENMENT

Foundation is basic striking and cutting technique and enlightenment is the deeper understanding of the strategy behind all things.

In most schools they try to separate what is taught to the beginning students from that which is supposedly secret and reserved for advanced students. In strategy, there is no difference between beginning and advanced. In combat we all fight with everything we have, and the outcome is based more on how hard the student studied than any secrets that were passed on to him.

In my school, I start the beginning student with the same cutting and striking techniques that he will use throughout his life. As his understanding of the true way of strategy develops he will become more polished. As I watch the student's progress, I determine when he is ready for the deeper teachings and I instruct him accordingly. My goal is to teach students in a way that they can readily understand as I guide them toward their own enlightenment.

In this world, if you start at the base of a mountain and travel far enough, you will find yourself on the other side at the base of the mountain again; you are still at the base of the mountain, but in a completely different place. This is the same for any path of study. You start at the beginning and struggle uphill. You go deeper and deeper into it until you find yourself on the other side with a heart of understanding. This is the way of all learning, and it is the only path to enlightenment.

Understanding this, I do not hold back knowledge from my students because they have not trained long enough. Each person is different and understanding comes differently to each of us, so I try to gauge the student's level of understand and teach each one what he is ready for at that time. I do not like pledges or oaths of secrecy. There are no secrets. Knowledge is open to all, but few truly want it. There is no need to hide things; most people go out of their way to avoid truth.

With this in mind, teach the students everything they can handle and hide nothing, because very few of them will ever come to real understanding anyway. Leave the knowledge in the open and only the true warriors will find it. Give them everything you have and help them past whatever shortcomings they have. The teacher should help the student come to his own enlightenment. Only this way will the student truly know strategy.

In this Book of Wind I have written nine sections on the teachings and philosophies of other schools. I could have gone deeper and pointed out details of each school, describing their foundation teachings and their supposed secrets, but there is no need for this. They argue themselves inside these schools over these points, and I do not like engaging in pointless arguments. In this book I discussed the major philosophies of each school of thought and pointed out why they were wrong. That is enough.

The only secret to real enlightenment is to keep your heart and spirit true, work hard, and be honest with yourself. Truth is not true because you want it to be. You cannot bend truth and still reach enlightenment. You must accept truth whether you like it or not, and adjust all of your views to fit accordingly.

The Book of Emptiness

The essence of my teaching is summed up in this Book of Emptiness.

Emptiness is that which cannot really be understood or explained. By knowing form and following strategy you will come to rely on emptiness, but it is impossible to fully understand, because it is spiritual.

Of course, there are no physical attributes to emptiness, and you can only come to know it by studying things in the physical world.

People have wrongly placed things they are ignorant of in the area of emptiness or the unknowable, but this is false teaching; it is based on a complete lack of understanding and it is an excuse for ignorance.

In the way of the warrior there are many fallacies and wrong teachings. Some, after being led astray from the truth, place the false things they have been taught in the area of the spiritual, as though no one could truly understand it. This is a lie and no warrior should ever settle for it.

For the warrior, the path to enlightenment comes by openly and objectively studying all forms of martial arts, sticking to the true path of the warrior, allowing no dishonesty in your heart, sharpening and trusting your intuition, and diligently practicing and clinging to the truth. In time, once the clouds of confusion have cleared, you will come to true enlightenment.

Many think that they are on the true path of enlightenment some through religion, and some through education. But true enlightenment can be seen by what a person has done, not by what he says. Those who have missed the mark may chatter all day long about this and that, but they have never done anything. Anyone can make a good argument, but few can show good results.

Understand all of this in the light of objective understanding and honesty. Practice hard and follow the path of the warrior without wavering. Keep your mind open to all things and always be straightforward and honest with everyone, especially yourself.

In emptiness there is only good; there is no evil. Emptiness is living by reaction rather than worry. To reach emptiness, you must study and strive for wisdom and endeavor to understand strategy. When all things work by their own accord, this is emptiness.

Miyamoto Musashi
May 12, 1645

About the Author

D. E. Tarver holds black belts ranging from 2nd to 7th degree in seven different styles of Japanese and Filipino martial arts. He has taught martial arts and strategy for twenty years. He produced and starred in the very popular *The Dojo Floor*, a thirteen-episode show on various aspects of martial arts. He joined the National Guard at the age of seventeen with his parent's permission and then transferred to the United States Marine Corps at the height of the Iran hostage crisis. Since his honorable discharge from the Marines, he has spent time in Japan and the United States.

References

1. Author, "Title of Article," *Name of Website,* Date, <http://www.geocities.com/georgemccall/early.html>.

2. George W. Alexander, Ph.D., *Miyamoto Musashi: Japan's Greatest Swordsman & The Book of Five Rings* (City: Publisher, year).

3. Wayne Muromoto, "Name of Article," *Name of Website*, Date, <http://www.koryubooks.com/library/wmuromoto1.html>. Entire article reprinted with permission of writer and publisher.

4. Earl Hartman— http://socrates.berkeley.edu/~cdea/JCAC/Kyudo/Book4.html

0-595-30124-X

Printed in the United States
25128LVS00007B/58-75